By Marsden Hartley

Adventures in the Arts (essays, 1921)
Twenty-five Poems (1923)
Androscoggin (1940)
Sea Burial (1941)
Selected Poems (1945)
Eight Poems and One Essay (1976)
Cleophas and His Own (1982)
On Art (essays, 1982)

THE COLLECTED POEMS OF MARSDEN HARTLEY 1904–1943

Edited by
GAIL R. SCOTT

Foreword by
Robert Creeley

Black Sparrow Press
Santa Rosa ᴏ 1987

ACKNOWLEDGEMENTS

Individual poems and "On the Business of Poetry" in this book appeared
originally in the following publications: *The Dial, Contact, Poetry,
American Caravan, Others, Others for 1919 An Anthology of the New
Verse, Contact Collection of Contemporary Writers*, and *The Triad
Anthology of New England Verse*.

Grateful acknowledgement is made by the editor to the National Endowment for the Humanities for the Research Project Grant which made possible the compilation and preparation of this edition of Marsden Hartley's
poetry.

Frontispiece: *Marsden Hartley, ca. 1941*. (Photograph by Louise Young,
daughter of Katie and Joe Young, with whom Hartley lived in the summers of 1940–43, in Corea, Maine.)

LIBRARY OF CONGRESS CATALOGING-IN-PUBLICATION DATA

Hartley, Marsden, 1877-1943.
    The collected poems of Marsden Hartley, 1904-1943.

    Includes index.
    I. Scott, Gail R.   II. Title.
PS3515.A795A17   1987   811'.52   86-26338
ISBN 0-87685-681-4
ISBN 0-87685-680-6 (pbk.)
ISBN 0-87685-682-2 (deluxe)

To
Aileen and William Hillman
whose light and life inspired this book

Contents

TWENTY-FIVE POEMS (1923)

BACH FOR BREAKFAST (1923–1929)

PROVENÇAL PRELUDES (ca. 1925–1929)

LAUGHTER OF STEEL

OBLIQUE FRONTIER

NEW RAINS WASH DOWN

RITES OF PASSAGE

ANDROSCOGGIN (1940)

Photographs appear after page 160

Foreword

YEARS AGO, when I was importuning the ever generous Dr. Williams for some contribution to *The Black Mountain Review*, he sent me, among other things, "Two Pieces," the first of which was called "Beginnings: Marsden Hartley." "Beginnings" of what, I wanted to know—of Hartley's extraordinary genius as an artist? of a time in the world? of Williams' own insistent flowering? Characteristically there was no simple focus, but the details and the affection are very moving:

> In one way I am not at all the man to write of Marsden Hartley. I know nothing of his sea-going ancestors, his down-east background. For that very reason, perhaps, since he spent his life, while I knew him, in an escape from that, seeking as a painter of pictures, to follow a life not as far removed from his hereditary one as might on the surface be indicated, I knew this phase and sympathised with him in it. He was in addition a poet, a writer with a delightful prose style which fascinated me. Besides I had had a father of the same remotely English blood who looked like Hartley, at least to the length of his nose, a nose, Dad used to say like the Duke of Wellington, a Roman . . .

One finds the same tone of warm respect in the way Williams remembers him in the *Autobiography*, clearly a man he was much attracted to over the years.

It is Hartley who brought together Williams and Robert McAlmon, which meeting led to an intensive friendship and the crucial magazine *Contact*. Hartley contributed to its first issue. Again and again Hartley shows up, so to speak, in the annals of the period as when one reads this passing reference to him *qua* explanation in Gertrude Stein's *The Autobiography of Alice B. Toklas*:

15

We were fond of Rönnebeck [a German sculptor who was Hartley's particular friend at this time] and besides the first time he came to the house he quoted some of Gertrude Stein's recent work to her. She had loaned some manuscript to Marsden Hartley. It was the first time that anyone had quoted her work to her and she naturally liked it . . .

His rapport with active contemporaries is very impressive and they range from John Reed to Alfred Stieglitz, his primary dealer at 291 (1909). There is a lovely snapshot of him sitting with Pound and Léger at the Dôme in Paris, 1924. A year earlier his first book, *Twenty-Five Poems*, had been published in the same city by McAlmon as the Contact Publishing Company, whose other ventures included early work by Stein and Hemingway. He appears in the definitive journals of the time, *Others, Poetry, The Dial, The Little Review*, et al. Yet such a simple image of success is deceptive, and some sense that he shares in the intensive literary definitions of the period—as do Pound, Williams, Marianne Moore, Stein or yet another friend, Hart Crane—would be untrue.

Hartley's poetry is specifically personal, an expression of feeling, a various response to the world *out there* he feels he can afford. It is also, in Emily Dickinson's words, his "letter to the World/ That never wrote to Me— . . ." Recalling the painful situation of his childhood in Maine—born in Lewiston, his mother died when he was eight, and four years later, after marrying Martha Marsden (the source of Hartley's subsequent first name, which he changes from Edmund in 1906), his father moves to join family in Cleveland, leaving Hartley with an older sister in Auburn, whose own family he not long after helps to support by leaving school early and getting a job in a nearby shoe factory at $3.00 a week—one must think that his art, no matter its sources otherwise or its exceptional gifts, has a great deal to do with what one can call, albeit loosely, compensation, an attempt to gain psychological respite or balance. For example, the family itself as a human term had almost fetishistic resonance for him as a letter of an old friend, Adelaide Kuntz, makes clear:

> The last time I saw Marsden was on a hot summer Sunday late afternoon, just before he set off on his last visit to Maine. He had lingered late in town as if loathe to depart and as if saying many wordless goodbyes. We met by chance in the Museum of Modern Art and I had with me my son, then sixteen, whom he had known from the time he was born, but had not seen for almost a year because the boy had been away at school. Marsden was overjoyed to see him again, and now almost a man, and very formally invited us to dinner "out of doors on a terrace." He finally decided to take us to the roof of his hotel, where we dined in the sunset overlooking "the towers of New York" which he loved. He seemed completely happy and proudly introduced us to some of the inhabitants of the hotel as we went to and from our table. "Now they can see that I am not just that weird lonely man they have thought, but that I have a family too — May I call you that?" It was infinitely touching to me, especially as I sensed his pride in being able at last, after all the years of fear of spending, to entertain his friends with some lavishness. I shall always remember him like that, with his extraordinary gaze steadfast under the glow of the late sun in his face . . .

The prosody of Hartley's poems is also "personal," which is to say, it is primarily his own invention, the heightening of a prose line so that it can move with the flexibility of music (which he loved indeed). The way he turns in (*plows under,* I want to say!) rhyming is fascinating in its effects, and his ear for cadence, especially in the late poems, is very articulate:

> When the surf licks with its tongues
> these volcanic personal shapes, which we,
> defining for ourselves as rocks, accept
> them as such, at its feverish incoming —
> isn't it too, in its way, something like
> the plain image of life?

Those restless entities disturbing solid
substances with a curious, irrelevant,
common fret — . . .

("Indian Point")

I recall first seeing this poem sandwiched in between those
of Eliot and Robinson Jeffers in Conrad Aiken's Modern
Library anthology, *Twentieth Century American Poetry*
(1944), and finding it then, as now, unique.

Hartley emphasized markedly the objective resources of
art, both in painting and in poetry. He was defensive concerning any sense that art came of itself, without an intensely
conscious deliberation. Yet in a 1941 letter to McAlmon he
writes: "All my poems are written first draft and left." That
apparent ambivalence as to whether one's art is deliberately
or intuitively made is especially familiar to American artists,
and the more so if, like Hartley, a large part of their
background has been self-taught. His training as a painter
was one thing, but as a poet he had only his own interests
and instinct to guide him, and he clearly felt a vulnerability
pertaining. However, his feelings are never absent in any instance of his art and like his hero, Walt Whitman, he so places
himself in his poems that "Who touches this book touches
a man . . ." As he says in "The Business of Poetry," a
magnificently various discussion which he published in
Poetry in 1919: "We present ourselves in spite of ourselves."

It is, then, this curious, reflecting voice that becomes
so moving. Its authenticity, of course, is immense and it is
both intensely local and universal at one and the same time.
Its size is intently human, thinking the world into meaning,
piece by piece. Again his friend, Mrs. Kuntz, says it most
aptly:

He was not really a talkative man — but he saw more with
his blazing blue eyes than anyone I ever knew, and he
thought constantly and he wrote a great deal. His mind
functioned with little rest — he told me once that he always
kept pencil and paper by his bedside and that when he woke

18

in the night and couldn't sleep, he could write down what
he was thinking. Marsden Hartley was an honorable man,
a really loyal friend . . ."

Here he can speak for himself.

Robert Creeley
Waldoboro, Maine
July 30, 1986

Editor's Preface

THAT A PAINTER OF THE STATURE of Marsden Hartley should also write poetry is not such an extraordinary thing. Many visual artists are able poets on the side or articulate spokesmen for their work. Some writers also paint with varying degrees of competence. The example of William Blake, one of Hartley's idols, comes most immediately to mind. What is extraordinary in Hartley's case is that, despite the fact that he is famous as a painter, and that he published only sporadically, he took his writing—both poetry and essays—as seriously as his painting. His habit, established over a lifetime, was to divide his working day between the two arts: writing in the mornings and painting in the afternoons when the light suited his needs. He was, however, more private about his writing and the first to admit the difficulties of braving the fearsome publication jungle. It was painful enough to maintain satisfactory relationships with art dealers, seek new ones when necessary, and continually push for exhibitions of his paintings with the hope of resulting sales.

Thus for simple reasons of exposure, Hartley is still relatively unknown as a writer—and this in spite of what, for a painter, could be considered publishing success in his lifetime: one book of essays (*Adventures in the Arts*, 1921); three volumes of poetry (*Twenty-five Poems*, 1923; *Androscoggin*, 1940; and *Sea Burial*, 1941); numerous essays and poems published individually or in groups in some of the most respected journals of his day (*Poetry*, *The Dial*, *Contact*, the *Others* anthology for 1919, among others); as well as the posthumous collection of his poetry, *Selected Poems* (Henry Wells, ed., 1945); and the recent volume of his essays which I edited, *On Art* (Horizon Press, 1982). In fact, Hartley's reputation as a writer reached a peak rather early in his career—during the late teens and 1920s when his work was first and most frequently being published, and he was most actively involved at home and abroad with other well-known writers—William Carlos Williams, Eugene O'Neill, Robert McAlmon, Djuna Barnes, Hart Crane, Waldo Frank and Paul Rosenfeld, to name a few.

It has been argued that an individual cannot, in fact, successfully pursue parallel careers in two such distinctly different fields as literature and the visual arts. Given the demands, amply demonstrated in Hartley's own case, of simply staying alive on the sale proceeds of his paintings, it would seem a Herculean task to undertake a second career. Yet Hartley *did* write—regularly, with enormous energy and passion, and with measurable publishing success.

But the purpose of this collection of his poetry is not to prove or disprove a theory about dual abilities among artists and poets in general and Hartley in particular. What occasions publication of this book is a desire, as it were, to provide the goods—to do what Hartley had not the wherewithal to do: find a sympathetic editor, and a publisher willing to champion the voice of one who is not primarily known as a poet. This book celebrates that indefatigable poetic voice, which refused, in the words of his own poem, "Oblique Frontier," to be drowned out by the "sea swell," but which "shall have empirically then / been made clarion—". Given their due place in the public ear, these poems will, I feel certain, not only prove their worth as literature of rare intensity and delight, but will also enhance our estimate of Hartley's overall creative achievement.

Hartley's voice was, indeed, "empirically" evolved. He was an experiential poet, a primitive (a quality he valued highly as many of his essays on art and literature attest) in the sense of being unschooled and largely self-taught. "I have," he wrote Henry Wells in 1943, four months before his death, "no culture in the academic forms. I have never felt it necessary to acquire all that baggage—I have let the divine mother of poetry itself show me the way, and if the real forms are there it is only because I must have absorbed them like a sponge" (Wesleyan University Library). Experience was his "divine mother of poetry," teaching him in no systematic manner what he needed to know at a given moment in his life. Blake, Donne, Emerson, Whitman, Emily Dickinson, Francis Thompson, Yeats—all the geniuses who were his poetic mentors—he discovered and "absorbed like a sponge" on his own. He had little patience for what he characterized as the airless poetic erudition practiced by his more illustrious contemporaries, Ezra Pound, T. S. Eliot or Wallace Stevens. Early in his career he turned instead to his New England predecessors, Emerson and Dickinson, as models; he wrote a poetry that emerged from the ecstatic reverie of the imagination. Later, in the true Whitmanesque tradition—with Williams, McAlmon and others—he sought a kind of poetry that pulsated with natural life. He experimented with a highly charged, sometimes bitterly satiric dadaist mode. And still later, after his return to Maine, his mature poetry breathed the stinging air of sea and storm cloud, and lamented with pathos the passing of life as seasons turned, and friends and fellow creatures died.

As some of his early correspondence shows (see letters to his friend, Richard Tweedy, Yale Collection of American Literature; and to Horace Traubel in *Heart's Gate*, Jargon Press, 1982), Hartley considered himself a serious poet even as a young man in his mid-twenties. Through the years he wrote prolifically. Some 600 poems and 300 essays are to be found among the Hartley archives at Yale University and elsewhere. Like his paintings, Hartley's poetry is rough-edged and spikey. This toughness is not, however, due to lack of skill in either poetry or painting. Rather it would seem that the rough-hewn quality of both poetry and painted image results from his desire to make an art with all the immediacy and varied texture of life itself.

This edition of Hartley's poetry is necessarily selective. Henry Wells, in his skillful editing of *Selected Poems*, culled mainly from Hartley's later verse, especially from the late 1930 manuscripts, and from the two previously published volumes, *Androscoggin* and *Sea Burial*. He included no early poems and almost none from the 1920s—not even those

23

which had found their way into print in *Contact, Poetry,* and elsewhere. Hartley's mature work of the last six or seven years of his life is, unquestionably, superior in its sweep of line and its elegaic lyricism, but the poetry of his formative years—beginning with the rhapsodic nature verse of his youth, continuing with the experimental dadaist work, the other poems of the post-war period including those written during the long decade in Europe (1922–30)—is crucial to a complete view of his poetic endeavor and informative as a parallel to his paintings in those years. The present compilation, while maintaining selectivity, has broadened the historical horizon to survey the important early and middle periods as well.

Despite his peripatetic existence (as an adult he never had a home he could call his own) and his living out of trunks and suitcases most of his life, Hartley's masses of manuscripts remained relatively intact after his death, and most are in the Collection of American Literature in the Beinecke Rare Book and Manuscript Library of Yale University (hereafter referred to as YCAL), though there are carbon copies of many of the manuscripts in the Special Collections of the Bates College Library. Hartley's niece, Norma Berger, was literary executrix of his estate and after his death made typescripts from a number of the handwritten manuscripts and helped to arrange all his papers. In the Yale archives her typescripts are clearly distinguished from Hartley's and have been used in preparing the present edition only for the purposes of verifying an occasional illegible word.

The Notes at the back of this book give details concerning textual sources, publication, probable dating, relevant biographical data, and information on related paintings or prose essays. Unless otherwise stated, all manuscripts can be found in YCAL. All poems which have appeared elsewhere in print, either during Hartley's lifetime or since, are noted; otherwise each poem may be assumed to be unpublished until now. In all cases where a holograph or original typescript (done by Hartley) exists, it constitutes the textual source for this edition. If only the published version exists, it stands as published, except for any obvious errors, which are specified in the Notes. If two published versions — but no holograph or typescript — exist, I have selected the one I believe to be closest to what Hartley intended. If there are discrepancies between a published version and Hartley's original, I have, in all cases, gone to the poet's handwritten or typed version as the authoritative source. In short, this volume is definitive in the sense of remaining as close to Hartley's original intentions as is feasible.

The effect of this editorial procedure may, to those familiar with Hartley's previously published poetry, result in what appears to be a less polished product. Both Henry Wells and Leon Tebbetts made editorial changes in the material submitted to them. Hartley seems to have been of two minds on the subject. Leon Tebbetts told me in 1981 that as he recalled, Hartley never objected to any editorial suggestions, but was only interested in the "look" of the poem on the page. Yet in his correspondence with Harriet Monroe regarding publication of the Kaleidoscope poems, Hartley pleaded with her to make no alterations (see Note to Kaleidoscope).

In past publications the most frequent type of editorial emendation was minor: punctuation, capitalization, and spelling (Hartley tended to use British forms like lab*our*, theat*re*, etc). Like Emily Dickinson, he seems to have balked at using normal punctuation. In his handwritten manuscripts, he generally used a variety of dashes: a small one could be a comma or a period; a large one could be an actual dash or a period; he sometimes inexplicably used a semi-colon at the end of a stanza when the sense called for a period. (The same odd habit appears in his prose where he might end a paragraph with a semi-colon.) But when one compares a holograph of a poem with Hartley's own typescript, many of these dashes become normal commas and periods, though often still used unconventionally. On this matter, he once told Stieglitz that he claimed to use no punctuation in his poetry "except the natural one of the rhythm it gets when it is read rightly" (letter to Alfred Stieglitz, March 15, 1915,

25

YCAL). In these habits he is again following in the Whitman/Dickinson tradition where the poetic voice, rather than grammatical or syntactical rules, governs.

Both Tebbetts and Wells added quotation marks (Tebbetts used single, Wells, double) and replaced some dashes with commas, periods, and occasionally semi-colons or colons. They also altered some capitalizations. In this edition, these changes in punctuation and capitalization have been restored whenever possible, according to Hartley's original, though to avoid tedium such variations are not specified in the Notes; only major alterations of spelling, added sub-titles, or textual errors are mentioned. Periods and commas have been uniformly placed inside quotation marks, which was Hartley's usual habit, although he was not always consistent in this detail. Words that Hartley had in all caps but which both Wells and Tebbetts italicized, have been returned to all caps.

In a very few cases where Hartley misplaced a beginning or end quote, or omitted the period at the end of a poem, I have silently corrected the error. Also, he had a habit of putting a period after the title of a poem; these have been deleted. Hartley uniformly misspelled words like "homliness," "lovliness," and "lonliness" all of which have been silently corrected. The form of one of his favorite words, "extasy," he probably derived from John Donne's poetry where it appears as "extasie"; in this case, I have let Hartley's spelling stand. Minor (typographical) misspellings have been silently changed; other types have been cited in the Notes. Foreign word accent marks have been added for clarity of pronunciation; Hartley almost never inserted them. An occasional grammatical error has been corrected silently. But all such editorial emendations have been made only when deemed essential to clarify the meaning of the poem.

Hartley habitually collected groups of poems together under thematic titles, and sometimes these compilations remained intact. A few collections, like *Altitudes* (ca. 1918) or *Pressing Foot* (from the late 1930s) have disappeared altogether. Often, especially in later years, he would gather

26

poems from different "books" into new arrangements, so that one poem might appear in two or more locations. Among the papers found in Hartley's rooms at Corea, Maine where he died, are some notes which appear to be a rough outline of section heads for a new book of poetry and are in fact very close to the division titles Henry Wells eventually used in *Selected Poems*, indicating that perhaps they had discussed these ideas when they met in the spring before Hartley's death. But in the final compilation of the book, Wells' placement of individual poems did not necessarily coincide with the manuscript collections.

Because the present edition seeks to remain as close as possible to the original sources, my effort has been to maintain the integrity of Hartley's collections by publishing those poems under a given section title which appear that way in manuscript. "City Vignettes" is the only section that borrows one of Hartley's titles and includes poems from other places, but I have stated the origin of each poem in the Notes. Also "Early Poems" and "Miscellaneous Late Poems" are generic section heads, drawing from a variety of sources, details of which are spelled out in the Notes.

Hartley told Leon Tebbetts that he didn't want his poems to be illustrated with his paintings, that he wished to maintain the integrity of the two art forms. There are, indeed, many enlightening and beautiful parallels between poems and pictures, in both particular examples and general artistic tendencies, and it is generally *expected* that these be shown together (as Henry Wells did to a limited degree in *Selected Poems*). I have, however, chosen in this volume, to respect Hartley's wish and to let the poetry stand on its own merits. Hopefully, with the greater availability of the poetry, studies of these rich correspondences will follow.

I wish to express my deep appreciation to certain individuals who have helped to make this book come alive, and to acknowledge those institutions which have had a part in its generation. Christopher Wagstaff spent many weeks poring over all Hartley's poetry to assist me in making a preliminary selection. His sensitivity to Hartley's best poetic

27

voice was invaluable to me. I am especially grateful to my husband, Stanley Scott, for his clear vision of what is possible and for his enduring support of my work, and to my son, Ryder Allan Scott (it is no coincidence that he bears the name of Hartley's favorite painter) for sympathetically allowing me to monopolize the computer to complete this work. I wish to extend thanks also to Townsend Ludington, Gail Levin, Gerald Ferguson, Katharine Wells, John Tagliabue, Ted Enslin and Robert Burlingame for their encouragement and enthusiasm for this project. Leon Tebbetts kindly shared with me his memories of Hartley and lent me photographs. This volume is a tribute to him and to Robert Burlingame and Henry Wells for their early recognition of Hartley's talents as a poet.

I wish also to acknowledge the National Endowment for the Humanities for a generous research grant (1977–1980) which made possible publication of this book—as well as my collection of Hartley's essays, *On Art*. I am indebted to Yale University for permission to publish from Hartley's manuscripts, and to David Schoonover, Curator of the Yale Collection of American Literature, and his predecessor, Donald Gallup, for their assistance in fulfilling my needs over the many years of preparation for this work. Kathryn Hargrove Lattanzi, Curator of the Treat Gallery, and Mary Riley, Librarian of the Special Collections at Bates College, have helped me on numerous visits and with many requests. Finally, I wish to acknowledge Norma Berger for her kindness to me and cooperation in my efforts to publish these writings.

Gail R. Scott
Presque Isle, Maine
April 1986

The Collected Poems of
Marsden Hartley
1904–1943

EARLY POEMS (1904–1918)

Light of Night

Orb of all pervading light
taking thy sure and gradual flight
adown the ages. What might
is thine, what sight hast thou
cast light upon: Dawn of never
ending day doth shine resplendent.
Thou are dependent still for day
to end to fill the earth with
mystic night. White those rays
of thine and bright, wondrous light.

Nature

The cinnamon rose doth
bloom so close to my
south window that bees
do rumble in and fill
my humble house with free
and ever pleasant music.

They shamble up and down
the tiny window panes and
tumble all about in vain
to fly away to freedom
and thus they stop and mumble
to themselves over their seeming pain.

They stop and rest upon the
bars as if to stop and meditate,
to rest and deeply think about
their plight when once again
they take their maddened flight
and out they go to the blossoms'

honeyed gate and then they prate
and preen their tangled feelers,
and state their sorry case to
those who happen to be near
and fill them all with fear
lest they too should be imprisoned here.

The rose doth only smile and
waft its ever delighting odour
across the warm and sultry air
with never a care for thee
but shares her sweets with all
who do but choose to greet her.

Sweeter far she seems to be
and all her buds do beckon me
to test her essence full and rare:
There doth she but rest and behold
the modest violet fleur-de-lis
which rests in crystal carelessly.

The clouds are slowly moving by
in tones of sad and sorrowing grey.
The sun doth shed its gentle light
upon the rose's glowing heart so bright.
The butterfly does greet the happy day
with its delicate airy flight.

The bobolink does rise, and sink
into the soft and feathery grass;
Its notes are like a gurgling crystal spring.
The pipe it plays on is such a delicate thing
that it great wonder and surprise doth bring
as it doth rise and its marvel of song does sing.

The Royal Love Child

"There is no life worth living"
said sad and troubled Sorrow:
"None but Poverty to lead the way,
Remorse doth follow in my step
and there is no peace of heart.
Tribulation plays her part in this
struggling strangling strife and
there is no hope in life."

And Sorrow passed along the
weary and darkened road: Death
did goad her on with his melancholy music to the brink of
hell's abyss. A stranger
with soothing voice and joyous
words did approach disheart-
ened Sorrow and with gay

laughter and happy smiles
did stand. Sorrow lifted
with her trembling hand the
banded veil from off her
brow and said, "Who are thou,
I have not seen thy like before:
Fairer sights than thee have
I never seen move:" The air

did play sweet music upon
Aeolian harps and the
stranger joyous said "I am
Pleasure and some do name me
King of mirth: Earth did
sing a happy measure at
my birth: Dearth doth
vanish at my command and

all the land doth breathe in
peace; Shall I release thy
soul from prison?" Sorrow faint
and weary said "Yea, if

thou canst make the morrow
brighter by thy presence I do
gladly follow at thy command."
And so did Pleasure take the

Hand of Sorrow and they wandered
through the land of joy. Hand
in hand they passed and
Sorrow rested weary head on
Pleasure's breast and life was
new to Sorrow; Saddened eyes
did brighten and Sorrow's
heart did lighten to the tune

of gayer song than she had
heard before. Death did
step aside and pay respects
to Pleasure. Remorse and
Tribulation fled behind when
Sorrow did no further comfort find
in their black and dreary company.
"Thou hast no further need to follow me"

did Sorrow say to them, and
they did vanish in the mist:
"List! List!" again said
Sorrow, — "What new and
stranger feeling is this that
springs from out my heart and
makes my blood's pulse start,
and what hand doth pluck my
heart strings?"

And Sorrow and Pleasure sat
them down to rest awhile, and
Heaven did smile upon them
and from out the breast of
Sorrow there did shine a
golden light, and light
took shape and did drape
his limbs in heaven born clouds.

Crowds of gladdened hearts did
gather at the seat of Pleasure
and Sorrow his smiling bride:
A messenger did approach and
touched the heart of Sorrow and
of Pleasure. All the heavenly
choir did sing to a new and
happier measure and Pleasure

reigned supreme:—And in
the bosom of glad Sorrow
a child was born. The moon
grew still more bright at sight
of all this joy. The light of
earth did weave garlands of
happiness above their heads and
the Royal Child was Love.

Summer Evening

Ashes of rose
Fade in the east sky

    Thru the quivering poplars
    Sun flashed swallows fly

Broad the blue stream flows
Under the arched bridge

    Down the gleaming sun goes
    Over the earth's edge

      A flush in the sun's wake
      A ripple—behind a swan
      On the tremulous lake
      And the day—Is gone!

The Mystical Forest

Vastness was a silver dropper
Out of which this day came,
Glistening, an ambient dewdrop
That rounded glistening in a globule
Dropping slowly from the stem of time
Into eternity.

Looking through its crystalline gleam
Land and scene were for me
The filamentary petals of some candent flower,
Travelling dusted with the pollen of sunshine
Through intricate wooded ways
I went seeking.
The forest gleamed in the distance
Edged against a sapphire sky,
And its trees reached up limbs
That were passionate slender hands
To hold their leaves of burning crystal high.
Over it all was a soft sheen
As of baby flesh.

*   *   *

I saw a woodsman
Going with an axe,
A stone-hard purpose in his eyes.
White hares were slung across his back
And tears fell from their soft dead eyes,
Eyes, so pink, and so blue, when they played
And nibbled the yellow roots of colored shrubs.
Where every teardrop fell a tall tree grew
With white bark, and strange marks upon its trunk.
Why the trees were white I do not understand
Since the rabbits' eyes were so brightly colored.
Sometimes a bronze mastodon would come plunging
And break down the slender white trees.
He must have been blind,
Though he had one eye, only one,
That shone as brightly as the sun itself.
Perhaps it could not see things less bright than it was.

How well I remember the loquacious peacock
Who strutted before me as I was in a lethargic trance.
She came and put her cold bill upon my lips
To awaken me with a kiss as bitter as aloe.
As she spread and closed her tail
In a ritual manner, music sang in the air.
Her eyes were jades,
Her feet were stained with walking in rose marshes.
I was whitened by flakes of sunlight
Brushed from the glow of her glory.
Enroute to the springtime of new generations,
She told me,
She had become anaemic through bleeding with ecstatic fervours.
The day seemed wan with the pain of hearing her voice.
Her words hung themselves like crucifixes
Amongst the tedium of other words I've heard.

*　*　*

There was the house of prayer
Made of tall pillars of crumbling charcoal.
Only sick people came and went from this chapel,
Fearing that nature having distorted them
They could not trust their impulses.
The sob of curlews from the marshes
Sounded like a monodiac dirge in the chapel
And mingled with lachrymose prayers sobbed forth.
Few people remained here long.

There were the amorous cormorants
Which made love like balloons inflating.
I watched them until I felt myself
So swollen [with] their same amative desires
That I floated away on air,
And the winds must have been at my wish's command,
For I alighted where the compliant maidens lived.

Many lovely ones there were,
Clothed in rays of sunlight
Woven with the strands of their hair,
And falling in heliotrope and amber about them.

I had only to look at one of them intently
And she would loose her garment at the shoulder
And stand before me, saying:
"It can readily be seen we desire each other."
Never was there a purity like that of their yielding.

*　*　*

One minute I looked out upon a violet cold ocean,
That I could step across, but could not see the other shore of.
So little does space mean.
A moth, freshly upholstered in red plush
With pale green and purple designs upon its wings
And a sea-gull like belly,
Voluted around me, a gaudy, ephemeral aeroplane,
Over-inquisitive. A wave finally drowned it.

*　*　*

I drifted on an icefloe down a stream
That opened in the earth as I came.
Frigid with hauteur the iceberg sparkled indigo
So that spectric auras buoyed it up and down.
I peeped over the edge and saw water swirling
In a vortex of bronze green purple and red.
It seemed to me I could evaporate
Into that swirl of color if I kept looking,
So I speedily looked away,
And leaped from the iceberg,
Taking a crystal chip of ice with me
To make a stickpin for me on holiday occasions.

*　*　*

The caw of silver crows woke me one time.
They were in the golden maize,
And rice marshes that were on either side of me,
Come there over night.
Their singing stung my ears like cayenne pepper.
One crow looked at me with clairvoyant eyes,
Then flew away and I understood that I must follow.

He led me to a stadium where a matador
Fought a cinnamon bull,
Dancing before him clad in Mazarine and scarlet.

39

He was as light as a sun ray reflected from a mirror dancing.
At last the bull gored him and tossed him high.
Unless my maladroit eyes deceived me
The matador evaporated into mist
Just as the rainbow goes back to sky hue.
No sign marred the limpidity of the sky.
With a snort and a flirt of his tail
The bull charged the stadium
And striking it, faded in a puff of igneous haze,
Everyone laughed in a debonair manner.
"A fitting way to look at such things" I reflected.
And smiled. When I was serious again
I could see only an autumn leaf where the bull fight had been.
And the silver crow had left me alone. So I slept.
What else could I do.

*   *   *

One day—I am weak when I remember it—
A day that was white with intensity of passion
That has had every dreg whipped from it,
And glows—a Christ-glow—
Through the darkness of the centuries
Across the space of the universes—white, always—
I came to the meadow of the illumined flower.

This was the harvest field and season
Of rainbows, and of soft colorful dawns.
In the wind loose buds of young days blew
And the soft blossoms of suns
Were breaking from their chysallises.
From the fire in the center of the earth
And the unsheathed gleam of sunlight in the sky
Lights co-radiated toward one point,
Where the illumined flower grew.
Its petals quivered livingly,
Casting off a scentless effluvia—
I halted in quiet pain
That seemed to lift me high into space.
All odor, and music and color
Were caught here and held ecstatically suspended.
My will and intellect vaporized and flowed into the stream
That inundated the livid orchid with glory,

40

And buoyed my flesh so that it no longer weighed upon me.
I had become but a particle of phosphorescence
Glowing upon the daedal blossom.

When its lure released me I came away slowly
Thinking I had looked upon a face rather than a flower.
Whenever a ray of light falls across my face
I feel that a strand of hair from the head
of the illumined flower has reached out tendril-like
To draw me back, seeking tenderly to rescue me from reality.

But I will never go back.
The memory of the flower is too beautiful,
To efface by seeking the actuality which created it.
I dare not lose my dream
By too bold an attempt to have it more securely.

Canticle for October

with responses for the coming of the magical Tenth wave.

There is piping on the hills of Caledonia,
This morning!

In the aromatic efflorescence of this clear
Warm enfoldment, exists my most eminent delight.
The morning is multi-hued.
There are soft grey taverns to sit in.
Taverns in the depths of these orbits
Where golden spots gleam through lattices,
Bound with happy vines.
I gathered up flexible baskets of the delicate
Abundance of this new fruition.
The edges were lined with fresh sprigs of heather.

There is piping on the hills of Caledonia,
This morning!

Shall the word Amour—be permitted?
A thousand annuities of praise then,
For the permission.
Love is the talisman for the unspoken bliss
Between two having the signature of the dayshine
Upon their highest wave.

I strive with all the white tentacles of my mind
To wrap myself around each delicate offering
Tendered so exquisitely by one, who having looked
Into the dark mouth of cataclysmic ambition,
Smiles with the old cognizance of this incipient
Humanism.
Death softens the steel shell heart struggling
With conspicuous largesse toward belief.
Death has for once been decent in behavior.
The plant, so avid of the ascending years, blooms
Toward the new sunlight with zest of illumined
Impatience.
Smile then for me, cognizant one, if for no other,

Comprehensive of the immutable heroisms
Inherent in the day's demesne.
I would be aware of these smiles for an eternity
Of moments, turn from perishable gossamer
To lustrous entities shrouded with radiant
Persistence and duration,

There is piping on the hills of Caledonia,
This morning!

Yellow bees humming deliriously over the heathertops,
That was the cadence rising from the hills of Caledonia
When the ninth wave receded, majestically making room
For this supreme *Tenth* of ours.
It was fair for me emboldened with belief
The oldest legend of the years.
There was no impatience with the rain.
The breath of many an almost beatless hour
Was made palpitant again.
Frost bloomed on frozen windows like spectral gladioli
At dawn.
Tendrils with a chance will climb on any trellis
Of the wind;
Their grace, to them, is indispensable.
Shall we then, strip the pristine tendrils of delight
Together,
For the elusive agencies to come.
Incredibly sliding years?

Responses—with delicate diapason.

Salt of the sea on my lips, lifted from the shoulders
Of this night,
So brave with comprehension, crowned
With eloquent simplicity.
Voluminous, phosphorescent SILENCE leaned
With her new-washed salted cheeks;
Young planets dawdled iridescently around
Around our tingling feet,
Radiantly in unison.
Will she breathe the old deliciously tortuous way
Again,

This mistress of the ancient, inexplicable
Fantasie?

Give me the years, as they are fancifully called,
To inhale the fragrance of these new effulgent
Ardours.
Eyes—
That may collect like magpies
The golden spots gleaming through lattices
Bound with happy vines,
Finding them there as lanterns, for the many
Incommensurable dusks to come.

Lips,
That shall lift the bright coinage
Of the new morning
From these soft, heatherblown gateways
Pouring their redundant cadences
Upon my grasping, eager ears.
Hands,
That may hold those fragments, shaken
From wires of stiff winds,
Words from the kindest days that pass
Onward,
Into the dominion of the far
Austerity.

October will bear no other burden
Than multi-hued feuilletons flying with windy rapture
Toward winter, relieved of its white and stark
Uncharitableness.
All that is perfect, is cool and sweet and beautiful
To the aftersense.
These words are therefore, not dangerous words;
Cool, and sweet, and beautiful.

There is piping on the hills of Caledonia,
This morning!

So sings the golden chewink, upon the edges
Of the last sunflowers emblazoned with the flame
Of noon.

A flagon of the sun shall be drained.
Seeds are his special quest.
Seeds, with the heart of splendid germination
Bursting them.
Hours when the moths do not gather,
Awake, with their pollen,
Celestial fertilization.
There is always the bee of heaven
For these superior cross purposes.

I make pact with you then.
Pact for the great appointment
Upon the highest wave of the world.
Shall we ride the eminent apex of it
With the quality of togetherness,
Which planets indicate in their manifold savannas
On a wide, cool evening?

There is piping on the hills of Caledonia,
This morning!

Ironies out of St. George's (1916–18)
(British Military Hospital, Bermuda)

■

Shepherd of the morning,
wailing.
Anguished have I well
crushed with the spell,
saw this, my weakling herd
to death-throes conferred,
stood stark beneath
the shadow tree,
saw them die
speechlessly.
What shall I, shepherd
who cannot herd my lambs
or sheep,
and cannot sleep.

■

I am an island—
My mother was a mountain once
My father is the sea—
Somedays I hear my mother grow
And see my father froth
And frighten me somewhat.
They have so many other children now
I do not count—
Some are ships and some are men
Of no account
We lose them every day—
They say!
I have no doubt
'Tis so!
I can not grow
Because my father hates
My mother so.

■

She had a way of doing
What she said she did
Not like to do.
She had a way of killing
Through and through.
She had a heart that kind
That she could always find
A way to pierce him through.
She said she loved him
More than all the world beside
It was her pride.

47

■

Like ice his blood
and burning quenchless fires—
His star-consumed eyes—
trembling, every nerve
with catastrophic strategies.
Not slept for days
with terror of death's ways.
I shall not die a death like this,
the tortured captain said—
I could not ever sleep
down there in Jones's watery bed
nor tolerate those miseries.
I want the land,
and let them have the sea,
who want
floating eternity.

■

We are knitting now
night and day,
the idle women say—
Is it for the men at war
who are so kind,
or is it simply for
the summer wind?
What man shall wear
a coat of joseph-hues
who cannot wear
his shoes?

48

■

Just one more
at the breast, she said—
for when I think of more,
and what these labours are,
I do not think it worth the while
to be so weak and pale,
and when I hear them say
how awfully
the ships go down,
I think they need not strive
so to be born,
for what you have
you cannot own
for long.
The pain this side the grave
is keen enough,
for love.

■

Where should we go
while where we go
but iron rain does fall,
and grave damps nightly
weave a winding pall?
Why should we throw
us in the blackening sea
for love of majesty?
Heroics need we
for a day of peace,
if ever comes
surcease.

49

■

Red targets blowing
in the wind, way out
beyond the blackening trees—
O what are these?
O they are targets in the breeze—
each one when struck about
a thousand men go down and out,
down to the teeth of the sea.
What other shall there be
for them so free
of doubt,
no surer boon.

■

Blandly she lies
beneath this speechless sky
all black and watery;
How now surmise
her sudden destiny
with wind, and wave, and man
where caverns are
within some alien deep
to rock her sons
to sleep.

KALEIDOSCOPE (1918–19)

In the Frail Wood

Marie Laurencin!—
How she likened them to young gazelles
Disporting in a quiet glade, with their thin legs
And their large wondering eyes,
Full of delicate trembling—shy, tender, suspecting,
Furtively watching for the stranger in the wood.
L'Eventail exquis! la main d'ivoire!
Les yeux de gazelles!—glimmering, provocative
Magic tumbling out of them like bronzed hoops
Or circled ropes to dance with like gilded wire.
The hand touches a frail cheek, and faints
In its cushioned depths with the excess
Of its palloring fragility.
Light zephyrs hover over the edges of frail lace,
And roll from off dark coils of ribboned hair—
Great bird-swings poised at the nape of the childish neck
Setting out the white throat from the blue or rose shadow—
Blue, and a far cerise, with a gentle dove-like grey
Encircling them, covering them with mists of timidity.
Speak they in concert of a little girl's morning,
As she steps frailly out of the linen and the lace
That folded her young virgin limbs from the terrors
Of the monstrous undivulging night:
Stepping out upon the edges of a world too bright
With glinting facets of a diamonded despair,
Into the busy bustling world of young gazelles,
With their long thin legs tripping noiselessly;
Into the thronging glade of girlish hopes and fears,
In a harsh world where the folding and the unfolding
Of tenderly sequined fans makes a living music
For their anguished eye and ear,
And a wall to keep the beasty wolves from their fingertips
And the tongues of hummingbirds distantly

From their young and frightened throats.
I hear the hearts of little girls beating
Against the hearts of the young gazelles!
It makes a white commotion in forests of thick pearl;
And their young white fingers waver as would
Young jasmine buds on the fallen embers of the breeze.

Her Daughter

She was so young, so like a tigress,
Her large round eyes of jet and amber
Lanceting one through from edge to edge
And from side to side with a girl's ferocity.
Her hair was short, also jet in hue
With blue lustres in it, and her lips were round
And full, and her breasts were round and full,
And they shot through the black wool mesh
Great shafts of jungle fire out at one.
She made no other overture.

Following her, upon the bridge made of young trees
Turned so like dusted ivory with the heats and rains
And fogs, and early dews and mists—
Or, as one would say, blanched to a veritable white—
Her mother.
Her mother, shaded by a parasol, walked discreetly
So many paces behind her—so many paces,
Smiling at something, surely not this,
Smiling with a vague enthusiasm;
For she was too old to laugh heartily about lusting flesh.
She had no breasts now, and her eyes were rimmed
With gold, and there was no light and no heat in them,
Or any tendency to casual fervors.

But she was young, so like a tigress—
Her very large round eyes of jet and amber
Lanceting through one from chest to spine
And from scalp to heel with a girl's ferocity.
She had her lusty appointment with the sea.
Her suit of black wool showed all of that—
Her lips were not colored,
And her hands were pale—the mother had no breasts.
This was certainly a fair exchange for the sea.

Spinsters

October in New England:
They are the gargoyles supporting old buttresses,
These virgins that roam wistfully among the ruins,
Victims of an effete worship.
Some of them love their father,
Some of them love their mother,
Some of them love themselves,
Some of them watch for a sail
That will never skim their horizon.
They form the granite supports in the arches
Of old cathedrals and mausoleums with shut doors.
They hold the rafters up, whose lacework
Is the fluttering place of bats.
There is a spacious cobweb covering all their nights
With a dewless gossamer.
A stillness that is the speech of ice
Consumes their swiftly gliding days.
They mother the owl and nurse the adder
In their vacuous dreams.
Lost hopes run rivulets of despair
Down their parchment cheeks.
They are rushing eagles without a sky;
Their pinions are drenched, their heads droop
And they cannot soar for the beating of the rain.
Soon, and they will join their sisters the leafless trees,
Who stand like stone until the lightning strikes
Them to the mouldy earth, or a lusty axe
Fells them to the ground for the evening fire.
Delicious would the blow of the axe seem,
With health and vigor and lust springing from the handle.
Leaves are they that droop when the first frost touches
Their veins; they coil together and wither on the stem,
Swaying and swirling to the earth.
Their eyes are like lanterns in the depths
Of old cellars that are riddled with the years.
Deserted farms are they, with the good grain gone,
The flax spun. The fox eats the grapes, the deer
Pass furtively by on the edge of the dusk
For the sweet apples fallen from the once young boughs.
They search the cellar, seeking the hummingbird,

And find the cutworm on the beam.
Gargoyles of stone—soon the wind will have lifted
The furrows from your brows and cheeks, and hands.
Soon—when the work of the wind and rain are done—
You shall have the youth of the dust upon you—
Then you can run and dance and blow
And toy with the wind as if you had borne
Litters of laughing children.
The dust is your sighing place:
When you have finished with the mottoes
Of old gravestones—"here lies," and what was good
Graven in white words—
You shall yourselves have one!

Bats breed in belfries, hummingbirds on young boughs!
Spinsters, you are the gargoyles for high towers!
The burr of the chestnut hides the meaty nut!

Swallows

The Blueblack swallows with their saffron breasts
Punctuate the rooftree—and they make pretty commas
On the wires,
And place superb accents above the blowing corn—
How would it be to skim like them,
The surface of all things,
To graze the cheek of every beauty,
And press one's lips to the sky, with a sudden frenzy—
To dot the pale vowels on the pages of the sun
With swift points of beetle-blue;
They turn their breasts up to the sky
Swinging arrow-like, upon a skipping wind,
These countless commas with painted wings.

Local Boys and Girls Small Town Stuff

A panther sprang at the feet
Of the young deer in the grey wood.
It was the lady who had sworn
To love him,
That rose, wraithlike
From the flow of his blood.
He swooned with her devotions.

There was never one
More jolly and boyish
Than he was, in the great beginning.
Once his slippers were fastened
With domesticity,
He settled down
Like a worn jaguar
Weary with staring through bars.
The caresses that were poured
Over his person
Staled on him.
Love had grown rancid.
Have you emptied the garbage
John?

56

Salutations to a Mouse

If a mouse makes a nest
Of one's written words,
Is there else to do but accept
The flattery?
I have deemed it wise to do so.
I have thanked him
Sufficiently
As he scurried in and out
Of the room.
He has faced the winter
With a nest of my words.
I did not suspect them
Of such worth against the cold.

Fishmonger

I have taken scales from off
The cheeks of the moon.
I have made fins from bluejays' wings,
I have made eyes from damsons in the shadow.
I have taken flushes from the peachlips in the sun.
From all these I have made a fish of heaven for you,
Set it swimming on a young October sky.
I sit on the bank of the stream and watch
The grasses in amazement
As they turn to ashy gold.
Are the fishes from the rainbow
Still beautiful to you,
For whom they are made,
For whom I have set them,
Swimming?

The Flatterers

I

The cactus has grown young leaves
One and a half inches long
Since I came to live with it.
Its branches are like the claws of crabs
In a bed of seaweed.
Young rosehued shoots are coming
From the new green leaves.
I have divined their desires.
They would make huge boughs
Of soft green for you and me
To sit under,
And tell each other of ourselves
And of the world.

II

Outside the wall of this room,
The young tamarisk tree waves
Its feathery grey branches in the wind.
It has sent its coraldust blossoms to the ground.
They were like wafts of smoke from a tepee
In the morning just before the sun
Reaches the desert.
I sat one evening in the moonlight,
Under the tamarisk tree,
And listened to songs from the lips
Of a Mexican boy.
He told me afterward in broken English
The meaning of these songs.
I could have told him a richer meaning.
I could have told him of your presence
Inside the wall of this room.
I told him nothing of your presence.
It is enough the cactus and the tamarisk
are knowing
And you, and I.

SUNLIGHT PERSUASIONS (1918–19)

Saturday

You, yellow climber,
You, whom I have the honor to address
Amorously, at the high noon of my morning,
The Sunday of a new caress is over me.
Just there, a little to the left of your cheek—
Sitting upon the needlepoint
Of an unfeathered plum-tree—
So high it is where he sits
The hills graze his eyelids and his mouth—
A mockingbird, amorously inveigling.
If you think he is mocking you, yellow one,
Do not trouble.
He is nevertheless
Singing.

With fan-shaped petals of cerise
The ground is covered this morning.
The ladies must have dropped
Their modesties here, last night—
In passing.

It is of them too the mockingbird sings,
Toward the morning.

The Topaz of the Sixties

In the little tired spring,
Weary with the years of bubbling,
Deep down to where the gold sand comes to light
Again,
I see wreaths and wreaths of smiles.
"L'amour quand-même!"—
The gold bird in the cage exclaims.
"L'amour quand-même!"—reiterates the lark
To the dahlias and the petunia buds
In the garden.
"L'amour quand-même!"
Sings the nightingale in the plum-boughs,
Where the clematis shuts the window in
With fragrant fringe.

Once it was a precious stone—
Long, long, ago.

To C——

I

If a clear delight visits you
Of an uncertain afternoon,
When you thought the time
For new delights was over for that day,
Say to yourself, who rule many a lost
Moment in this shadowy domain,
Saving it from its dusty grey perdition,
Say to yourself that is a flash
Of lightning from a so affectionate west,
Where the clear sky, that you know, resides.
The rainbow has crossed the desert once again,
I took the blade of bliss and notched it
In a roseate place.
It shed a crimson stream—
That was our flush of joy.

II

They will come
In the way they always come,
Swinging gilded fancies round your head.
So it is with surfaces.

They will walk around you
Adoringly,
Strip branches of their blooms for you—
Young carpets for young ways.

With me it is different.

Stars, when they strike
Edge to edge,
Make fierce resplendent fire.
I have lived with bright stone,
Burned like carnelian in the sun,
Myself;
Myself seen branches wither.

Carbon is a diamond—
It cuts the very crystal from the globe.

You are so beautiful
To listen.

The Asses' Out-House

Three flies lay sleeping
In a cobweb shroud,
Dreaming of molasses, of jam,
And of heaps of offal.

The fourth swung by his ear.

He was a withering fokker
on its last tail spin.

His body was bluebottle;
His wings were grey
As his cobweb shroud,
Stitched with prism hues.

He was dreaming of old bones
On which to rear his young.

The Festival of the Corn

(The dance is given on the fête-day of San Domingo. The saint's wooden image having been venerated in the church of the pueblo, the procession now emerges, carrying it into the plaza.)

> Dance, Domingo, dance!
> Give him a leaf of corn in his hand;
> Rub him with blue corn-juice —
> His legs, his hands, his arms.

The black horse and the ochre horse
Were prancing on the front wall
Of the little mission.
The dark red boy sat upon the roof,
Waiting for the first gunshot
> To strike the hammer on the bell.
With ribbons they brought together
The new brides and bridegrooms of the year.

Fantastically they rose from the kiva,
The koshare; with cornhusks on their heads,
Cornhusks of the year that is gone;
> Rabbit's fur for girdles;
Orange corn for necklaces.
Turtle-shells, sea-shells, and ox-toes
Made music like juvenile xylophones
> In the wind.
Their bodies were naked but for the breech-cloth.

> Dance, Domingo, dance!
> Give him a leaf of corn in his hand;
> Rub him with blue corn-juice — his legs,
> His hands, his arms.

They came with the shot of the gun
From the church, bearing Domingo
Under a blue calico canopy:
Priests in robes, acolytes in overalls,
Little red acolytes with bluebottle hair.

From the kiva-side the drums began to beat:
Men of the chorus were gathering.

They sang in unison, resembling old choir-boys
In the organ-loft of the mountain-tops.

One by one the youths of the Domingos
Came up out of the kiva's mouth,
Beautiful as young girls at maypole time;
Their hair combed and oiled with bear's oil
All the way to their waists.
                    Jet, with the reflection
Of eagles' eyes upon it;
                    Jet, with morning blisses reflected;
Black rivers of young hair, striped with rows of blue corn.

A girl, a boy, a girl, a boy, a girl.
A man, a boy, a man, a boy, a man.
Long lines of wondrous dark flesh
Turning toward the ash-gold dancing place.

                    Pom, pom, pom, pom, pom, pom, pom:
The rawhide drum was muttering, as the macaw
Feathers of the ceremonial rod waved
                    In the summer wind.
Crimson macaw-tails, and a coyote's skin
Were trembling to the aria of the young corn.

They sat him down, the still Domingo
Of the wooden soul and the stove-pipe halo,
Gilded with store bronze.

                    Give him a leaf of corn in his hand—
                    Let him dance!
                    Dance, Domingo, dance!
                    Jesus won't care,
                    For a little while.

Up the long plaza step by step, with red-man syncopations
In their ears, their red feet trod the way, coercing
                    The adolescent corn.
They want the young corn-breasts to fill with young milk;
They want the ear to hang heavy with orange and blue milk.

It is you they are singing for, young corn! It is for you
they are dancing, the red young bodies flushing with an old
flame of the sunset. The red of the west is coming up
out of their loins, up out of their boyish and girlish breast-
flanks. Red sparks are falling from their carved lips.

Dance, Domingo, dance!
Rock the young Jesus to sleep.
Lay him down under a candle.
He'll drowse and fall to dreams with the thud-thud
Of the beautiful red feet on an ash-gold earth.

Green corn-leaves, evergreen leaves, ox-toes, turtle-shells,
sea-shells, and young bells ringing at their knees. There's
the pagan hymn for the ragged Christ-child.

Mary is picking field-flowers on the edge of her blue robe,
behind the adobe wall of the church. Domingo sits under
his calico canopy waiting for oblations. You, lovely red
boy, pick the paint from his cheeks, and let the old smile
through to the sun. The sun will crush his lips. Domingo
wants to dance, children of the flaming west.
Domingo opens his wooden eyes.

Beat of the tom-tom in my ears! Thud-thud of multitudinous
red feet on my solar plexus! Red fire burning my very
eyelids with young red heats! The last saps of the
red-man are pouring down my thighs and arms. The
young red blood is dripping from the flanks of laughing
red bodies aching with the sensuousness of the passing
pagan hour.

The blue milk is rising in the cornfields. Can't you hear
it rising like new fountains from the old mother breast?
Can't you see the little trees of blue milk spreading their
branches on the sunlit air?

Sky-blue and corn-blue are mingling
Their kisses like the rainbow edges
Of a whirling spectroscope.
Blue prisms dangling from red bodies—

65

Blue corn-juice dripping, drop by drop,
Over the edge of luscious young red lips.

The mother is granting her favors. The father is blessing
his corn-children with celestial fermentations. Blue milk
is rising from the ground; pouring up through the cornstalk
fountains; dripping from young corn-leaves. Red lips are
spreading trumpet-flowers—ready to catch the corn-juice
as it falls.

Statures are increasing. The red-man boy is growing an
inch taller before my eyes. Something is coming up out of
his ruddy breast and thighs and arms.

Something is reaching out over him.
          It is the blue corn-juice
His mother is pouring over him
          Soon—there will be ribbons of new
Marriages stretched in front of the altar rail.
          The old choristers are singing
In the organ-loft of the mountain-tops.
All the valleys are in unison with the thud-thud
Of multitudinous red feet.

The Jesus-child is smiling under the candle
At the feet of Domingo of the wooden cheeks.

I saw you, dance, Domingo. I saw them rub blue corn-juice
on your legs, and hands, and feet. I saw you step down
from out the candle branches. I saw your heavy feet grow
light when the red boy smiled you away from your calico
canopy.

Dream, little Jesus-child! The sunlight from little candles
helps the pagan dream. The red boy laughs your grief
away—with his young luscious body. The fountain is
filled with the blue juice of the corn.

          Domingo nods with heaviness again:
          Straighten my stovepipe halo once more;
          Take up the posts of my calico canopy;
          Carry me to the altar again—

Back to the Nottingham-lace curtains,
And the blue robes of Mary.
The Jesus-child is waking.
Stick the old pap in his mouth—
The pap with the milk that is grey.

TWENTY-FIVE POEMS (1923)

World-Passport Visa

I was born on the island of New England.

Had I not escaped to the continent,
Joined the elephants and tigers and acrobats
                                        of New York City,
Which is the greatest circus arena of the world,
I would be chopping twisted trees
                    to clear a space for calm,
                                persistent contemplation.

I was sired and damed by Lancashire.

The continent I visited, became
                        a village in distress.

I saw the mountains and the trees
                        grow small
                                with patient subjugation.

I had lived with trees,
                Had seen the wind grow gray
With harsh inefficacy of effete
                                dramatic mood.

My forest had become the world,
                With grinning branches, under which
                Hot legs must dance to tunes
                        consistently evolved,
                                for purposes intended.

My citizenship is never questioned, as I pass—
Because I also dance to comic tunes
                Made ready for the stiffening heart.

68

Who smiles, confers a rain-check
                         in an untoward hour.
Who frowns, confesses immediate misconception
                              of the game.

A cigarette must perish in a dish
                    Made beautiful for ashes—
                                   edged with gold

An almond brown, submerged in chocolate
                              removes the taste
Of too much roast, with sauces
                         indiscriminate.

The Fork of Annie

One of Annie's forks is doing time
in a summer wayside inn today.
The other five are somewhere else, or maybe
There were twelve in all. Most people hope to have
a dozen with their knives.
There was a day when Annie had a home
with things in it to be proud of—a sewing-machine,
a sink, two tubs, a boiler, a bench, the pans, the pots
That every stew is used to, with all the other things
that lie around, as any new young woman starting out with any
    new
young man would have. The Saturday's receipt would get them
on their way. There is the time for pride, and that's
when everything is new.

Annie did her own and sometimes other people's work,
for when he was away at sea, the days came on, one just like
another, leaving little difference for Annie, all alone.
Something must be done with most of them, for everything
gets used to everything, when little is the shape and growth
of everything.

Annie didn't have the way men like when they come home
from thrashing with the sea.
Women grow old, women like Annie grow old, when men get
    quickly
used to what they do not find in them. Men get used
to everything in their women.
One of them wasn't regular, so someone said, and someone
always knows. Someone said it was a gale of wind
took and kept him,—someone said it was a woman—when
he didn't come again. Someone said 'twas Annie wasn't
regular. Some others wouldn't tell.

Love is blind—it goes, and there are things to make things
change and change.
Annie's name is carved across the fork in calm spencerian,
just "Annie," that is all, and there is only one of Annie's forks—
The others went some other funny way—things will get turned
around, lost, twisted, changed, mislaid.

They do not tell what made the change, or why the forks of
     Annie
went the way they went, or why he went away, and stayed.
Some said it was a gale of wind, some said it was a woman took
and kept him when he didn't come again.
They only know that something brought a look in Annie's
awful eye. They know the tree they found her on,
and say that something wasn't regular, they're sure.

Are You There, Rose Trumbull?

Having searched in every vain crevice of his hopeful imagination
For the sinful inkling of her face,
His letter was returned on him. "Not found,"
Was all there was to intimate the reticence of
Rose.
She had remarked once, "I shall be in Oklahoma
For a long time; I know I shall adore it,
In Oklahoma."
Rose Trumbull must be all [w]orn out by now,
For she was saying less two years ago than she would like
To say, —
The rakish ranchman proffered this dry touch
To every far loquacity.
Some deaths are slow, and dust is dust,
And wills to blow—and blow.
"Take this desert, how do we know who it is,
With all its windy vagrancies clogging up our doorways,
Settling down on everything."
His spurs were clinking out the same sweet tune.
He kicked a hollow ox-skull that had lain long
In the sand, in the sun, neighbored with young mesquite
Boughs.
A rattler was crawling through the socket of an eye,
The eye farthest from the sun.
He kicked the skull again, thought she might be there,
In the steel blue shadow underneath the heaviest jawbone.
Rose had learned to hide from him—he said.
But dust is dust. Is that you, Rose?
Or maybe it was Rose, making the golden ring
Upon his sombrero of thick brown velours.
Maybe it was Rose upon his window-sill.
Dust is dust, and dust will blow.

How blustery it becomes in recollection
Of old names.
And what becomes of all our evening tricks,
Our elegant atrocities?

72

Gulls at Gloucester

Hours in themselves are fiercely umbrageous,
As anyone in perfect comprehension of them
Will testify.
If their ways seem like folded tents of terror
It is certainly because they have taught their wings
To fold with beseeching calm in the face
Of fascination.
If you watch them for an interval of short
Or of long duration
You will come to the very certain conclusion
They have listened to the blackest words
That have rushed from the stiffened phrases
Of frightened men.
This may account for an obvious whiteness
Of tone, and I fancy there is something too,
In the quality of this white, of the brave
Capacity for endurance.
Experience will show anyone the way, pointedly,
To hold a mouth like a shut tent, and a desire
To fold or clench the hands from too much
Wilful glee, too much of anticipatory bliss.
So it is, I seem to feel that certain hands
Fold precisely in the manner of brown and white
Gulls' wings, after the sea has given up the blackest word
That is utterable.

Cobwebs and Ratholes

Do not ever let the door of the old garret creak
for long.
Leave the musty flax all twisted there, on the worn-out,
useless wheel;
The hoop-skirts, the almanacs, the iron mortar,
All in the blue grey places, leave them.
Hedgehogs have homes among them, with reminiscences
for pastimes, for weary, winter afternoons.

"Lead kindly light, amid the encircling—"
Someone is looking, someone is looking out of the window,
Between the edges of the Nottingham lace curtains,
Something neither wild, nor tame;
Is it ape, or armadillo, or is it simply—
COUSIN?
Seatowns are like inland towns,
They have their innuendoes.

Knotted fingers come, through, just over the edges
of the curtain, adders' tails wriggling through the scallops
of cheapest lace,
Cactus thorns, scraps of old horns left in the barnyard
to wither with the indolence of sun.
The hand pinches a white calla-lily flower;
The yellow tongue in it stiffens with amazement.
It sees two idiot eyes peering down into its white mouth.
The idiot loves the sick smell of calla-lilies,
Loves the skin of his nose scraping against the velvet
of the lily.

Gloxinias, fuchsias, begonias,
All are crisping with terror, curling and crisping
with plum-blue terror.
The purple eyes of the idiot are SETTLING—on them.
What are you doing there, Jonathan—is the cry from where
Pigs' parts are being boiled.
COUSINS—what shall be done with them?
They must never be left alone with calla-lilies;
They tear them with their stiff horn fingers—
They cannot stand the white-indecent innocence of them.

They twist them—twist them—twist the very
tongues out of them.

"Lead kindly light amid the encircling"—
Take that rope away!!!
Don't you know idiots love ropes—
Ropes and rafters, and lilies' tongues!
Never leave the cousins in a place alone.
They cannot stand the length of what they see.

Boston Portrait Projections

Corillyn is Dark

Corillyn will come, with her accustomed tricks,
To you for tea, an inauspicious day,
And one may even decorously say
She's always there quite inauspiciously—
But she is one who always has her time for play
Of her eccentric inhibition.
"I'll drop in softly as a morning dove—
At four or five or six—
I can't precisely tell just when or how I mix,"
Is what she dearly loves to offer for her certainty,
No matter what you wish to prove or disapprove.

The things that from her swift incessant tongue do fall
Like bullets having no restraint at all
Shall add no little to your quaintest miseries.
She's sure to put you somehow in an awful fix
With what she's sure to tell or never quite to tell;
You almost want she shouldn't stay.

She'll come, this Corillyn of theirs, not "yours,"
Like rabbits hopping to their mouldy hutch
When hounds are smelling at the gateway of their warren walls
Too much,
And take the bloom from all your foliating hours.
And there will fold around your clammy brain
The fungus-smoulder of her dark insinuating touch.
She'll leave a brown residuum on every corner casement
Of your altercating strain and make you never want her there
And make you want to curse quite plain.
And you will surely move your cold disintegrating chair
Because you touch in her the origin of pain.
Corillyn is very, very dark,
And scrapes your tenderest branches of their bark.
It's not because she dotes upon her arguments—
She is merely such a flagrant, vagrant one
For whom no thing can ever quite be done,
To whom encouragement is never sent.

The ropes of her inelegant precisions
Will coil about your calmest, simplest hopes
Like spirals of thick visions
In a small-town cinema.
She'll turn your cups of efflorescently informing tea
To vehicles of green and grey nostalgia,
For which there's nothing left to do
But put one's needful terminations through
With burning tropic eye.
And as you watch her watch, the cakes will change
To wafers in a helpless rage
Like worn-out actors on a failing stage.

It's not so much what Corillyn will put you to,
As what she always does to what she leaves with you.
There is another timbre in the room
That makes you hunt the broom.
But Corillyn is clear, with all her jocund
Glacially engendered heights,
As altar windows in an old forsaken choir
Wherein one icy word has been too bold;
And in and out of all this brown and bluish gloom,
She takes you through her caves all hung with stalagmites
That drip with frigid milky dews, wherein blind fishes
Have a dome.
And then you rush to pull the chain of every creaking transom
In distress—
You call a cab, and draw on gloves, with press
Of other business.

How brave it is of Corillyn to live,
Is one of many thoughts that swarm upon your sense.
If one could only entertain the half that girls like Corillyn would
        give!
So meagre all these portemonnaies
of recompense!

               *   *   *

Rapture

Is the confession of the leaf—at the brave moment of trembling. The white virginal ones run long thin fingers through the mystic's fiery hair. It gives a slight twinge to the gelid existence of the virgin, about to perish. This virgin is male. Is the spiral eligible, when it comes too late? Take me with you, upward fire of the man—swirl me away from ethical ethers. Swirl me from this arterio-sclerosis of the soul. I am not known here. I am not known there. I am not in reality known outside myself. God does not covet originality. The virgin twirled a bit of pointed lace that festooned his illicit mind, and settled down to more opinionating at the rusty gate. The university whispers—the mind is carried in another bag, and weighs too heavily with mystic themes on hands not made for work. The lunchroom notes the bookworm fattening its lean body with flesh of other minds. The lunchroom notes the pity of faggot gathering brains. The classroom loves its bag and worm as arums love the sickly tropic shade. The white hands turn the leaves of other minds and wander whitely in the world of other men's appraisals. They never redden with their own incisions in the flesh of proud experience.

A gathering of words of other fondled words begotten is called investigation, and this in turn is called cerebral rapture.

Asceticism is a virtue in itself, the boyish virgin says. It saves a lot of trouble.

* * *

This lady rides a languid dromedary toward her dear-God

She being most zealously in love with her
                    conspicuously PRIVATE
                                        afternoons
when the monetary makeshift lies on the horizon
          like a medal of the inefficient combat
                              of the ragged years,
all best honours effaced
          through stale, most irrelevant custom—

taking on all the irrationalism of an unexpected
                                    fever—in a quite
                                              indifferent taxi,
she fainted with due regularity before its terrifying
                                    orient floridity.
I will attempt no more translucent pyramids—
                                    she wistfully remarked,
making her spinsterly decision colossally distinguished
                          for its starkly obvious simplicity.
Her veils tormented the hollows in her blondine cheeks,
calling for the usual overladyish gesticulation
                                    of her wiry hands.
She had seen GOD once, or so she presumptuously thought,
(false ethers floating in a not too average brain)
washing his own cracked porcelains in a much befuddled kitchen
showing here and there a onetime nacreous resplendency—
(there lay the awful truth to cover)
Amid the musty odour from the butler's pantry,
exhausted cigarettes of the centimillions of those none too well
born guests who made themselves at home with stilted density of
    soul.
The servants of this most illustrious house, to which, so many
said in times gone by, it is great honour to be invited,
from which to[o] many unengraved returns had come—R.S.V.P.—
those sharpest words of all
Had gone to watch the pale blue ivy climb above steel graves
of those who perished for the then so unrestricted huge idea—
And THERE—the master of the house was seen—ALONE—
making notes, with whispers on the side, of all the spoons his far
respected guests with gentleness had lifted in their moments
of ineffable simplicity, with jasmined hands to keep swift hounds
from tracking royal bijoux to those shadows where deep pansies
take another purple for their thought.

          She wanted all the world to know, though not
          too safely know, she did not really care
          to ride the way she rode, with too conspicuous largesse
          but dromedaries are notoriously kind, she said—
          and wait with desert patience for the work they have
          to do with every day's humidity.

I ride this way, because I feel there is for me a MISSION—
beneath some golden escalade
                              SOMEWHERE,
where maids of better families may have the proper
                                        housemaid's knee
to make the way seem brighter than it ever was
                                        for THEM.
It seemed to her that all this hoping in the air,
might bring her to that vastest door a mind had ever made—
        "I'll find the key through thought, one day, for thought
                            is EVERYTHING—
                    some venture to expose so wilfully—
the day is young, though I am thirty-three"—And with these
flagrantly repeated words would feed the humpy beast
With ginseng leaves from which cheap substitutes for opiates
                                        are drawn.
        A cognac has a kick, SHE knows, but not for long,
        and snow is merely white, and temporal.
        But ladies of this ilk are never, never sure,
        and so her afternoons are long, though, entre nous,
        she quietly confides, not ever long enough for what
        she has to do, when pyramids are seen like points of glass
        on horizons too hot for vain prevision of inane
        resplendencies like hers.

Diabolo

Dedicated to the James boys,
Jesse, Henry, and William
and especially
to the twitching nostril
of Henry—
as well as to the honest-to-God look
in William's eye—

These three James boys have done
the delectable work of the world

Hold-upsscalpel-like impudence
of the imagination—
and a perfect fund of damning
the prevailing systems
of
EDUCATION

(Written especially for the Society Anonyme and read for them
at their DADA evening meeting, 1920)
IMPORTANT—to be read any way
it is possible.
Each to his own.

DIABOLO—
I have many playmates—
POPOCATAPETL, ORIZABA, VESUVIUS—
MATTERHORN—one cheek gone.
I have many playmates TERRIFIC.
From the mouths of my playmates
I have wound
whole skeins
of
FROZEN whispers
Bequeathed them
by
DIABOLO—
Popocatapetl, Orizaba, Vesuvius—
Matterhorn—one cheek gone.

Ring around the rosy—on a crater's lip—

81

Tea this Aft?
    Playmates—thunder jugglers—sky drunkards—
sodden night shoppers—
    crusty window lifters—
        blackjackers—snowbirds—
benders of street lamps of illicit
          IMPASSES—
    feather tossers—dream throttlers—
swinging gourah fans—
    wind biters—
    kissers of icebergs—
        osculation DIABOLOICAL—

Madame POPOcataPETL
        will pour tea   this aft—
from her own hospitable
        fujiyama tooth—
ring around a rosy
    on a craters lip—

POPOcataPETL is pouring—
    with lava syrup in it—
    to sweeten it—
    dynastic tea—
        INFORMALLY—

We've been lying, climbing, juggling, throwing the javelin,
    bending, twisting, receding—
    GRINNING moist grins—
In an African apricot jungle—
while the white epidermis of
      POPOcataPETL
    melts with livid afternoon fervour
DRIPPING
    new driplets for
      Cousin marmo—cousin goril—
        cousin ouran-outan—

I have many playmates
      pretty-pretty-pretty—
    WHIPS for witty ones—
      lion's-leopard's-ASP'S
        TAILS—

Harpswoonish fishes
            swishing
                  CATTLEYA   corselets
      with impertinently voracious
      SIP, sip, sipping—

I have many playmates
                  popocatapetlorizabavesuv—

ULIVI—
      Sister Eva   TANGUAY
            will shake lust dollars
                  from her playful light blue
                              hip pockets—

      HOOTCH
            from her fanatical
                  roTUNDities—
            Sister Eva
                  will tell the world
            a basketful
                        of
                        insidious (something or other)
      SIMPLICITIES
            shaken out of her ABASHLESS
                  reperTOIRE—

DIABOLO—
            ring-around-a rosy
                  on a CRATER's lip—

POPO has a tooth loose
            from which pour BLOOD and FIRE
            in—promiscuous—
                        communication.
            Steam hissers—lip kissers—
                  watch all brakes, joints, ratchets—
                  WRIST WATCHES—pistons.
                              bearings.
                              hubs.
                              tires.
                        MONOCLES.

ULVI
       is testing the tooth
            of
               POPOcataPETL
                  with ultra red needles

POPO will pour
         TEA—
            this afternoon—
              SEISMICALLY
                from her
                     one great hag's tooth—

    Ring-around-a-rosy
             on
           A
            CRATER'S
                  LIP—
   DIABOLO—
    DIABOLO

The Crucifixion of Noel

The situation is blue and white,
Inevitably.
High on the snowy hill, cramped with persistence of the frost,
Stands the little tree, all smiling with blue fruits,
Trickling with moss, made of tattered strings
Of moonlight.

Blue fruits, from the October of infinite twilights,
Ripe fruits fallen from the lush branches of renascent skies.
Blue fruits,
Cheeks of pale ladies, overcome with wakeful worshipping.

I saw them fall one evening, from "her" cheeks, when the
        mountain
Of her love approached.
She was all blue then, all blue with height of sky submissions;
It was autumn time among the icebergs.

Blue plenteousness,
Multitudinous curves of white parapluies
Overtaken with shower-lusts of the new summer afternoons.

What a beautiful harvest, I ventured.

Persimmons from the highest branches of the midnight
Of the south,
Leaning toward the mouth of the infant,
Orizaba.
Eyes from under the brows of the over-credulous;
Snowladen foreheads of both sexes, pallid with faith
In fiercely imagined joys;
Virginhood in its time of glaring,
Flaring certainty.

Sunbrushed antelopes leap in and out of the fervours
Beyond the light blue boughs.
On their young velvety horntips—steel coloured birds
With clipped, radiant plumage, sit fanning out their wings,
Whispers of many a commiserating dusk.
The airs that hum have the hilarity of Aurora's smile,

At the blue apex of midnight.
All about the branches of the Noel tree
Pass buoyant funerals of rainbows,
Aged with pain of summer.

Hush, baby of the incredible Friday-doom!
See! All the foreheads of the world have flashes
From the eyelids of the midnight on the pressed curves
Of them;
The girls and boys are dancing, with darts of dying rainbows
Impaled in the flesh of their knees.

I hear the ting-ting of the blue cymbals
Upon the white fingertips of the crucifixion crew;
They are floating—the ting-tings—
Over the breasts of adolescent icebergs
In my polar rendezvous.
A blanched cygnet glides across the frozen lake,
Under the Noel boughs.
The swan-child has in her beak a blue fish from the nets
of the night fishermen.
Cygnet's eyes are still blue fruits, and her back
Is strewn with clips of frozen sunshine from the virginal blue
    morning.
Ting-ting. Ting-ting. Ting-ting.

Blue raisins are dropping from the chilled boughs.
Ashes from the snowy hill are sifting into blue eyes,
And the wind carries the rune away.

Ting-ting. Ting-ting. Ting-ting.
A rope of ice has been stretched from the white earth
to the bluest arc in the sky.
The arms of Noel have been nailed with spikes of sapphire.

How white is Noel today!
Was he ever so white as in this last hour
Of his vanity?
Ting-ting. Ting-ting. Ting-ting.

Blue drops falling from sapphire nails,
Just where they pierce the white, white flesh of Noel.

Is there pleasure perhaps, in the dropping
Of the drops?
Little cymbal tones, falling in circles
Upon thick pavements of ice—
Noel is crucified!!!

The fishermen of the night are whispering
With the awakened ones among the nets—
Noel is beautiful in his new position.

Ting-ting.   Ting-ting.   Ting-ting.
The cymbals now have whitened.

BACH FOR BREAKFAST (1923–29)

■

B. is for Bach—
and all his noble sons,
who wrote square music for nave
and for loft,
for arch and for aisle,
for all the lost, forsaken things
no other sound will save—
Bach for the blest, who seeks no more
his peace,
but finds in this sure, square music
sound made logical—
solace for the swelling earth,
and climbing sky;
Sound—
that gives such decent reason
why a sound should be,
form in form,
logic overtaking the night,
setting the senses in a row,
perfecting the orderly march.
I never heard a stone peal forth,
I never heard a bell go crashing
toward the day,
the incandescent news to tell,
until the Bachs brought word
the very shape of things
to praise.

■

And, if the Popocatapetl
would have words, who can blame
His Majesty—if, after four hundred years
He should decide to shake the monstered tropic
to the very stem, and curl of every petulant tail
with sulphuric revisitation?
How really handsome the pageant of idolatry
must seem, in the city of the Amacamecans,
that sacred altar of the Chichimeca,
the dropped assumption of christian charivari
designed to disturb the ghost of Pedro Valencia
with piles of coloured papers, bunches of raw cotton,
locks of red and yellow human hair,
the hues of the insignia of the firegod,
embellished with fierce fresh flowers
from the amazed, and once placid fields of yesterday,
in the hope of appeasing this need of a quiet smoke
at His own fireside;—
And, if the holocaust should come,
sanctioning the aristocracy of Vesuvius, Mont Pelee,
and the so recently destroyed placidity of profile
in Fujiyama,
is it not merely a mark of accustomed sociability
among the members of the geological "Entente Cordiale"
in general,
and the subtle anxiety on the part of minor eclipse
or major constellation,
lest there be a dearth of ruin, on which to place
the ruminating eye, ever in search of a new patina
to imitate,
a "view" near which to subsidize a perfect speedway
for the oncoming flood of nouveau riche?
Must there not always be devised, new toys
to amuse the fresh, upspringing civilizations, in need
of new legends to recite,—
what happened yesterday among the Amacamecans,
after those four hundred years of the assumed
inanition of our friend in stark disguise,
His Majesty,
the Popocatapetl?

From a Paris Window—High

In this city
of the generous,
all are chivalrous.
It is a scene
where all are kind
unless the wind
be unkind
in blowing chivalrous release
over the unsuspecting mind.
It is a country
where the lip reveals
no bitterness
or irrelevant distress
unless
to be so secular
instills a sharp remorse;
it is a place
where no one ever sees
a face,
and yet strange bodies
meet
and speak an alien
sanskrit
in which specific comprehension
eternally resides,
and no grammatical despairs
are theirs.
Sunday is the day
when motley
sways
their way,
who come to speak a word
that never shall be heard
unless
it be, that silence
covers all necessity.

The Woman Distorts, with Hunger

Trees, just trees
imploring,
Let there be no more than these,
the bough against the wind,
the bole itself so kind,
explicit equilibrium restoring;
Her retrospect of men
so over-fetched, distraught,
by avariced implication come to naught,
calling for these far-deferred affinities
as one might yearn for bread and cheese,
so ample in themselves.
This wealth of proud satiety incurred
by means of word upon the edge of word,
Not really having learned the trick
of whipping whey from curd.

She saw, or thought she inevitably saw
among the high, sweet hills of home,
as in the nature of a welcome judgement come,
Herself, the old, wild road resume —
there being sense, proportion, sensibility
in "tree"
brave homeliness of perspicacity,
to cover with a glance so damascene,
this clipped, curbed hedgerow of her men,
conferring on their much too diffident brows
the correlated news,
to plant above their over busy eyes
these plain, irrelevant veracities.

A crutch, a willing crutch they come,
supporting up to every edge of home,
each elephantine arm;
a husband's *carte d'identité* she reads,
the while she ravenously pleads
for ways by which to reach
her bold, disdainful trees,
with ill, unsimulated suavities.

Trees, just trees,
and well she might incur,
with all her plaints of woman hunger
the swell of all these native boughs,
her broken fantasies to house;
The crutch she leaned so heavily upon,
was shattered all too soon,
till, one by one, recounting all
the monstrous inequalities, as withered
trophies taken in her jungle of despair,
nor finding any of them fair
as even "crutch" might willingly assume,
but one from off the hedgerow of her
counted men,
old thorn mistaken for the youthful bloom
because it gleamed with ancient amatory red,
whisked into comfortable usages
like remnants of a much too haggard broom,
her eyes cried out for old, dissimilar trees.

Trees, just trees,
she saw the deeper, wider, cooler
sweet amenities
among them, in the illkept regions
of her listless mind,
rhapsodic legions
of them regally resplendent,
kind,
where she might toss and tumble to herself
in every fitful maelstrom of distress
each flagrant aspect bless,
or curse, both being just, her broken thread
once more to bind
about her own emaciate limbs and head,
and wait for wind to shatter gossip
with fraternal wind,
among her covetous trees;
The bread and cheese would come
on every sobered mind,
as something plaintively determined,
the travail of the old road home

to be
her one complacent, dreamed
necessity.

Passionate Rebuke

One petal to her mind
more
than is allowed for symmetry
by the genealogy of this votive
botanical species—
and the movement all gone,
into the littlest hands
among women.

Whom, but this intricated self
could gesticulate to a simple little thing
of Bach,
and have it seem of one piece
with the sweep of an Andes bird
on the downslide for a spring lamb,
the soul of a cigarette in her shoes,
all smoking up—curling up, out
of the top of the tepee, beneath
her renaissance hair.

When I saw her in bed—in Hamburg,
hidden among the handsomest green leaves
her mind could foliate,
impromptu,
I thoght it expedient to summon
a physician for special devices
to save her
from the premature November
of her will.

She is steadier now,
than she was then—but I know
No one shall save her, despite
the dowry bequeathed her, at the right
time;
She will, in the end, perish, slenderly
respecting art, like so many others
of us.
I could have borne anything but this

at Rumpelmayer's—on a Sunday afternoon.
O parasitic dreams,
what a death.

■

Holding in reserve
a certain tendency to speed
accentuation,
mistaking nevertheless the pistol shot
for the race,
paying the huge penalty of ultra-previous
enthusiasms, love squashed flat
into patterns of adoration,
all flatness misconstrued for
serene quantitative—
"I see, in time, there is yet
time to make it round,
pumpkins in round heaps of fire,
bodies made round"
                his hat still sitting,
                rakishly,
                above his ears.

■

Come,
     tired old thing
     called morning—
straighten out your back hair,
get ready for business;
The clergy are opening the iron doors,
murderers to be conferred with
by appointment—
all hustling ladies having thrown
their combinations
in a corner,
garters in a curl,
grey hued leaves
impeaching vociferously
the overconfident vine.

■

These miracles of Paris
with its rues and faubourgs, lined
with doors that once were barricades
giving in suddenly, divulging
their broken songs;
Grenelle, Varenne, Villette, Menilmontant—
A frozen vocalist standing in among
the herbage,
porcelain blossoms in every shaken casement,
at every hinge,
mortuary chapels
of embalmed cafards, each with its lamp
of lightless oil;
unknown hero[e]s smiling calmly at their own
incognitos,
admonishing every footstep of this hour
to cease its foolish clatter
between persistent and consistent shafts
of rain,
dogging the peace of immemorial victories.

■

Tomorrow being Monday—
          what a piece of information it was
to cope with, regardless of the regularity
of them. This busy look on the washline
at ten in the morning of the habitual Monday,
after all, some high indication of the importance
of bodily piety, marking the repetitive beginnings
of the tame semaine, in times of
terrible slackness.
What is a Monday, anyhow, and what is a tomorrow,
and what, in the last terrifying moment
is this young man to do when it happens
they become one and the same thing.
The Alps know no Monday, and as for tomorrows,
they were so plentiful when I lived among
the redmen and the mexicans, it seemed ridiculous
not to have as many mañanas as the rest
of the world out there.
Ships do not sail on a Monday, among the majorities
of those that leave on a tomorrow,
at eleven, twelve, one, or two;
Is it, perhaps, that somewhere, in that strange cage
with the multifarious wings beating against
its impotent bars,
there will be one among them with the gift
for exquisite escape,
knowing a legend of the sea, or a tale
from the valley where tomorrow being Monday
has a history of its own,
Tomorrow being Monday, being the anniversary
of the fall of Messina, or the first still-born
child of an Igorot mother, or, more whimsical still,
was it perhaps this very Monday, when there was
to have been a tomorrow that Easter Island
was said to have gone under?
What shall this thing mean to any,
or all of us,
Tomorrow being Monday?

The Sister

Given the rock to hew, and split,
and carve, if she could,
some figure on its empty face,
with only fire in the pick,
by flaming heart updrawn—
From whence do these women come,
who fight the day down
over every thickening horizon—
bricks, mortar, and a frozen wall
of flattened dreams,
clover in the grass,
browned lilies by the lake,
with only fire in the pick
by flaming heart updrawn,
salt in the soul that helps to build
the sea,
from all the themes
the woman's will was made,
and her stout blood was tempered
to their tune.

Chirico—and There Are Blue and White

Horses and hummingbirds do not mate,
they have too much in common by the sea.
When shall be found the law, that brings
these two together in a common vortice
of consent?
Blue alfalfa for the pinto, and the mustang—
chariot steed must fatten on his stretch of blue.
Temples are the best of tether for a restless hoof—
the bird must buzz, until it find a home.

Cellaphon—a Favorite Word with Picabia

It will not be questioned that some men
find their paradise revealed on wires
with the position of the body reversed;
This hand-stand is not at all uncommon.
You will often come upon them in a sleek impasse,
Eyes sundered with a litter of stiff dreams,
faces appearing, as if by proxy, through the dark—
seeking for air from a window that is never
closed.
"Let them have air"—
And Cellaphon smiled,
and sang with softest ease,
an ancient Sunday morning hymn,
"There is a green hill,
far away."

■

These shells are paradox,
Carpaccio tells—
Peace issues from their lips,
the struggle with the sea
is now beyond recall—
sesame to ears
that seek a timeless refuge
from the wave,
and wind above the wave.

■

The beautiful rush,
breathing still the breath
of vanished crowds—
bloom on the breasts of birds
migrating from Madagascar
and the Easter Isles—
clips of light on stone
still clinging to my eyes—
strains from the busy hours
flooded with swift pains
of bliss—
multiple strong fingers interlaced
with whispering ones
forming walls of China
for the secrecies of those intervals
far too brief
and priceless in their brevity
sweeping the stakes away.

■

The eagle wants no friends,
employs his thoughts to other ends—
he has his circles to inscribe
twelve thousand feet from where
the fishes comb the sea,
he finds his solace in unscathed
immensity,
where eagles think, there is no need
of being lonesome—
In isolation
is a deep revealing sense
of home.

■

Life ahead, life behind—
echoes of the maelstrom,
and of dust that never falls,
trellised all about with vines
that shoot
and offer rich covert for thick moths
whose underwings are red, and black,
and red,
barred and circled with inquisition themes,
hints of the thing no fingers touch
or if they touch,
are washed of all their guilty smother.
Saffron
to the east bespeaks
a tender scheme above the tarnished steel
of morning in the mind
with chill perfections driven
to the sea, and there forgotten
with respect—
laurels to the wave that takes them down
to depths that smother them
consistently.

■

Being new inside—so that outside, the outside
shines new with it—life all sparkling on the
skin, so that when one is naked, anyone who may happen
to see shall say, "how did you happen to get that way,"
It all came from the shine of life that went in, and
came out to the surface again; And while it was in,
it did away with what life then was, and must never
be again.
The stupendous calm of Titian, unity, poise—
The wisdom of Leonardo,
That melting into the sun, of Giorgione,
The noble verities of Zurbaran,
Vision, reason, form.

■

A tree that bears—
waters its roots from the sky
that offers it the requisite
celestial moisture;
It is the earth that sustains
when skies are froward,
and uncertain.
Earth, the very best
of friends,
let my feet cleave to you,
and say to themselves,
Heaven is under me,
we are together.
Let me feel that I am one
whose feet are sure,
fit for the rock
and the cliff,
for the long, sun-glazed thread
called the road,
able to breathe the air
that earth exudes,
requiring no certificate—
mother and son, the best of friends
no false assertions of identity
intervening,
sceptical and suspicious.
These hands, that worked so hard
to pull the heavens down
now break crisp morsels
of sure earth,
calling them sky-emblems,
fragments of hope—
with the lure of reality
within them,
I say to you, smoothed pebbles
from the bed of the salutary Rhone,
My will is broken of its wilfulness
to climb the stairless air.

PROVENCAL PRELUDES (ca. 1925–1929)

■

Dusty olive trees
so dusty,
dusty with their own deep breathings.
Single little almond trees
along the Roman highway
from Béziers to Perpignan,
every little almond with its own shower
of congratulations,
oil in the very bough
exuding at the hilt of summer,
filling to the tip of the two-edged blade,
summer in the Rhone.

African cork trees
at the gateway of Port-Vendres
shedding their crusts of grey,
leaving behind them, round tusks
of cinnamon red,
from which thick branches lean
toward Afric winds.

Les Baux

Rocks chilled to whitenes,
frozen into white—
maddened with the two-edged blade
the wind,
with the terrors of battle
and the madness of young men,
whitened with the fierce tenacities
of the aged—
this two-edged blade
the wind,
turning every soul into a desert
of despair,
multiple agues of the aged
crisping every crevice,
every profile seared with merciless
chromatic hues;
rock demons,
and white neophytes in moods
and shapes of prayer.

As I stood leaning against this two-edged blade
the wind,
listening, bracing myself against this blade,
I said—
murder is a morning's premise
within these ashen walls,
among these stilled, forsaken caves;
wind
is the theme in every young man's mind—
wind
that shall take him to the brink
of mercenary love,
casting him over—
wind
that shall take a young man's mind
where innocence is forgotten;
Not among these rocks
can young men live, and keep their senses kind
dogged forever by this two-edged blade,
the wind.

The Bird, in Soliloquizing Voices a Woman's Wish

Where is the albatross at home?
Such questions trouble me at times;
Through what strange vistas does he roam,
and what are albatrosses' daily schemes?
Does solitude reveal a frigid bliss,
is north the way he looks, when dreaming
of release —
What kingdom of oblique recourse
can answer this?

No alien lighthouse
clipped with midnight bloom
but offers alien welcome,
as when he sleeps or wakes, there is not rock
or shore —
a country is not more;
To love the wind, and never care for peace,
to blink a weary eye on sinking ships
and heartbreak sighs of helpless men
upon their sightless way to dungeons
out of ken,
Are these an albatross's pleasure
then?

Has he a substance called a heart,
and does he yearn for love, when mists
come down
upon his waveworn town?

I heard a piercing shriek
from out the thunder and the freezing wind
that chilled me to the quick
of all my beating bone and blood
as only frozen answers could—
"These things are kind,
and prove the nothingness of things
beneath, or yet above my ceaseless wings —
I love this quest of nothingness"—
What answer, or redress?

"I only, heard the words he said"
the woman muttered
in her desolating plight —
O, that I could be,
so erudite.

It is the woman who supplied the image,
feeling, and thought herein expressed.
She seeks with earnestness, for everlasting
release.
How to live, and still be nothing—this is her
quest.   This woman is Norman.

Violet Grape—and Shadowy Myrtle Leaf

These glistening brown eyes that shine
as flakes of liver on a steel brochette,
deeps of brownest plush—grapes' blood
tinged with laughter, and with swift
douceurs.
Vineblessed voices naming little names,
Sweet recitations out of flame-red cradles issuing,
reflex of the earth itself—
where is there richer music on the wind,
Mont Espelido?

Touch me, brown eyes, dark of the darkest grape
beneath the vine
blue, brown, violet-black—
lilt of the morning on them,
Touch me, cover me well,
blanket me—
cover me well from the pain
of leaving soon
for other, stranger scenes.

Corniche — Marseille

These tarnished islands — set
in dictatorial blues,
Etruscan in their migratory hues —
the mystic severance reveals.
All islands have a faith in which
to rest,
keeping immemorial tryst
with integral tenacities.
How certain, that the morning is a myth
to them,
and night,
a casual theorem of conceit
where thoughtlessness of thought
can never intervene
within the geodetic scene.
This much has proven to be true
with such expenditures of blue.

Summer is done —
The mistral takes the theme
of summers
down beyond the edges of the sea,
transmuting them;
the olives are fulfilled.
The perdreaux skim above
the pungent gorse,
the newts and lizards seek
a lingering warmth of wall,
the junipers a multiplying blue,
the cigales sing
no more.

■

Solitude is kind
among these cool collines,
when mistrals do not blow.
There strikes the hour in every breast
when solitude is beautiful,
the bravery of moments come to life again
when pressure of irrelevant themes
bears down, and threatens to destroy
the living sense of them.
To be at last "within"—
ceasing to be those perishable blooms
of fruits and leaves—
the thing upon the surface
giving only shine
from other superficial things—
round, square, oval,
filling up the mould.

CITY SCENES (1930–35)

Window Washer — Avenue C

Before the greenish door she stood,
wild with insidious motherhood.
Her eyes and breasts were singularly small,
the rest of her was monumental.
"I cannot come on Friday sir — I'm jew,
will Sunday do?"
There was a beastlike strength in what she said,
the temple in her soul was hallowed
with an ancient, patriarchal pride;
A palestinian splendour rose
from all these elemental shows,
and what the ancient tablets say
is still a decent destiny.
I saw her window Friday night,
it bloomed with sevenpoint candlelight.

Bulldog on the Roof—Avenue C

Above these Lithuanian cliffs
and sunwashed, Polish shores,
I come to crowds of pigeons in a nacreous whirl
above these immigrational roofs.
The bulldog at the cornice just across the street
is wise and thoroughly discreet,
reveals a crazed, interlocutory esteem
for freedom unbestowed upon the ground;
In this the beast is very sound—
and what seem like morose pachyderms
possessed of adipose desires
are chiefly gastanks bulged with monetary theme.
It comes to this at two or three each day
disclosing unpretentious strategy;
The wash upon the line perspires
with vaporous effigies of labour and of lost desires,
domestic hatreds, and illiterate lust,
the wind blows up a prudish dust,
suspends dull arrases before pernicious eyes
that strain to gather up like sleek, immoralistic magpies
odd bits of scandal, little jokes, domestic perfidies.
The bulldog thinks the day is perfect,
and he, not being human, is correct.

Kuzan—First Avenue

Kuzan swings a wicked thurifer,
exuding sour frankincense and myrrh;
The smoke comes pouring from his lacerated eyes,
he mourns the death of fierce, ancestral destinies.
I look at Kuzan, as Kuzan looks at me,
and what I see is more than he can see;
I have no noble travesties within,
for I was born American.
He holds his head with deeper, loftier fears
and weeps ukranian, sacramental tears.
What comes of all this transpositional despair
reveals a surfeit of swift agony where
eloquent repose should be,
and Kuzan battles with an ultimate duplicity.
The serum did not take,
apparently.

Two Ways of Love

The father was a man
and he punished the boy-child—
this being the way of a man
with his boy-child;
For this the boy-child
never forgave his man-father.

The mother was enveloping—
she curled the boy-child's hair
in ringlets—
The boy-child grew to man-child
then to man,
and his curled hair grew down
to his heels,
and strangled him.

In Those Exquisite Areas

In those exquisite areas of isolation, one comes upon
the most priceless treasures.
One who seemed for long at the point of bursting, and
how many are there like that on every busy street,
bursting to the point of death for the need of
telling someone—SOMETHING.
Is that why we look at each other so searchingly, as if
noting buttons out of place, or spots on clothing?
What we really look for, is because it seems as if one
might tell the other something, or—fatality of all—
EVERYTHING.
The terrible siege was broken, as he said to himself,
I will tell no one—ANYTHING.
From that [time] on he seemed to be like another person, and
everyone began to notice this change in him, and to
praise the remarkable look in his face.
Daring at last to be alone, he was swept from his feet by
the tide of his transformed anguish, joyous with
the freedom that surrounded him.
I have at least learned to tell no one, ANYTHING.

You are looking so expressive said one, on a certain
Saturday afternoon—
and he knew that now he could long have what he long
had wanted.
He could be alone, and from then on his days and nights
were crowded with radiant events.
People wondered why he laughed, almost out loud, as
he walked.
There is, after all, a—PARADISE.

City Vignettes

1. Musicologist — Preference, Prokofieff

Her face is applewhite, just where the
worm lies asleep—
she has the terrible look of keeping
some secret tryst without weeping.
She is dressed in the very best of
very black
such as we often see when obsequies are over;
undoubtedly
her half-parisian blood brings this about.
The red glove on her tenacious left
denotes the passion of her frozen heart
the green one on her frigid right
bespeaks her intellectual birthright;
She has given all her soul to the love
of three oranges
which isn't in all, so very strange.

2. She Sauntered Most Elegantly Down

the aisle in an eastside department store,
you know, the one of the blossoming fields;
The long flowing robes made of rags, swung
regally, as the peignoir of a duchess;
She will lift something sooner or later
I said to the vendeuse, and it will not
merely be—her feet.
O ain't that awful the pretty vendeuse said—
O no—not really so—I said,
for life is just a little klepto here,
a little klepto there, a little klepto
everywhere.

It's been a damn bad day—no doubt the
klepto said,
as she stepped into her newspaper bed.

Daily Library Visitor

I seem to hear winches and peaveys
and capstans as he walks,
the great rumblings of a quiet man put
to good use—
he sits him down—reads nothing in particular
but looks like a monument of fine conduct
as he does it—
his field has been ploughed—he knows this
better than anyone else how many rocks he
took out of it
and how many worms came up for the robins
he has seen clouds of frozen breath rise
from oxen nostrils
and heard often the click of iron shoe
against broken rifts of granite,
and perhaps the impertinent laughter
of herring gulls above his blueberry fields
the laughter is not respectable which steals—
once it was anchor chains probably, then it
was ploughs,
now it is just fixing things up around the
house,
now it is the quiet look of a mystic in love
with a simple theme,
for the beautiful mask is utterly unruffled—
and the huge hands seem to say, we have earned
a little respite now, and can afford to hold
a book.

Window Cleaner to Nude Manikin

He being the big thing he is
needs lots of room for his
cleaning window tricks—
So they made the window empty
though they didn't take the naked
dummy out, she with her nose quite
some in the air
they often are so very debonair—
he swishing this way and that
with his window swiper.
He thought everything was very fine
when suddenly the naked woman
said—
big boy—why are you so cold to me?
Who's goofy now—the big boy to the wax
woman said—
this ain't no place for anything
can't you see for yourself it isn't—
besides I got plenty to do
I'm workin' for my cheese and bread
my job's washing windows just now
maybe later we could have a word
if things look so good.

Sweet Old Man

He wears a rose of celluloid in winter
upon his chilled lapel
for he is cold somewhat already
with pressure of the years on his chest
some days one sees he has had a hard night
of it staving off merciless and belated
dreams,
you know how a dog does when it lies and
dreams
with paws and nostrils aquiver
well, so it is this dear old thing seems
his bones are tired as he walks—
on days of spring he wears a living flower
it seems to give him power.

Un Recuerdo — Hermano — Hart Crane
R.I.P.

"Death thou has left behind,
the center of life is here;
no wounding needst thou fear
nothing can hurt thee more,
nothing can force thee or bind
thy self is no longer near;
no hostile voice canst thou hear,
upon this infinite shore."

Jacopone da Todi

"For when Urizen shrunk away
From Eternals he sat on a rock
Barren: a rock which himself
From redounding fancies had petrified.
Many tears fell on the rock,
Many sparks of vegetation.
Soon shot the pained root
Of Mystery under his heel:
It grew a thick tree: he wrote
In silence his book of iron."

[Wm. Blake, *The Book of*] *Ahania*
Chap. III, V.III

And, should it be left like this,
dear Hart, like this,
too much of fulfillment, no more promise,
given over petulantly, fevered,
you the severing, we the severed,
to wind-wash,
wave-flow, wave-toss and thrash,

beating forward, backward, to and fro,
in the unremitting high and low
in the never ending torment of today,
yesterday, so redolent of geniality—
never again to know tomorrow,
Atonatiuh crying loudly, augmenting our sorrow,
"what is life worth, if in the moment
it can be destroyed"—ancient Aztec lament
come over to us,
never a respite of tomorrow.

Wave is wave, Hart, wave is wave,
can it comfort to be wind-slave,
blow with the silence of the quasi-brave
upon a wide, unsensing mead,
heeding not death, or being dead?
Are they dearer for being nearer
to this bronzed outspoken earth
with its sandalled, molten mirth,
loved, cared for richly, this loud-lunged earth
so perpetually antiphonal, majestically antiphonal
to the crowded ear and shrouded soul?
Has it sense or double meaning
to be hushed, equivocally still,
seized and kept from sacred quiver
of delicious, sunlit earth-fever,
to be forever and forever
keepsake of so listless a lover?
Is it, is it, Hart, you find
it easier to give in to wave-din
freed of the harsh travailing of mind
fierce beating of the burning heart
and its veiled, surging smart,
seeking respite from the day and night
night and day refrain?

Loved you were, Hart,
surely you had well surmised—
you must have known, and prized;
It is not work to love
when the curved, rhythmic trace thereof
shines through, as bright light beams

through clipped obsidian blade
in warming, crenelated shade
white with unhindered orchestrating gleams
of morning with no obfuscating shadow laid
upon its never too promising brow, for the hue
and measure of love is not in cry and shout
but in sure-spoken unspoken certitude
without cheap subterfuge of bargain-hunting nonsense
never blurred with roistering word,
goodfellow-like, procrastinatingly inferred.
Love is love, Hart, and you were loved—
How could useless more be proved
in the round and round about,
and from us yourself have taken,
left us withered, worn, torn, shaken,
broken with the thought, we might have won
and you too have won, if you had sworn
the sane, same faithfulness to the sun.
Crash of noon, Hart. How could you see
it through with the gongs of midnoon clashing,
clanging welcome of renown
from azul-vistas and previstas down
huge blasts from the bellows
of the sun.
You knew them, yet could mistake
them once for dark insinuations toward
an everlasting dark, ineffable intake
from which no glib protest can glide
or childishly, or even manfully hide.
Earth wanted you, because she knew,
she always knows who has his cue
in place to be dictioned perfectly in space,
true inflection never falters, never alters
when the tone comes booming from the breast,
life discerns the rest, she knows and hears
above the monotone of roar and grind
each moment she herself be found
forsaken and foregone, she herself is pained
at losses never to be regained.
You had this lover, what more to be desired?
Earth hears the rumble of our thronged and sandalled feet
and finds their music sweet,

she craves
the tender, lustrous worship of her slaves.
In ebony and oxbone whitened in the sun
are you housed and harboured now,
symbolled of profusioned hours and what came —
white for a blanched and listless one,
black for the blankness, black for blame
of them that took you down, and kept you
wish or no wish, to drown.
Why should we be driven therefore, to condone,
left to condone a lecherous, treacherous prank
with none but instabilities to thank?
Oxbone and ebony and a vision neath a film
of cellophane, this was he, to say,
before he went away, and only yesterday
we had the genial bulk and blood and all
its amiable hardihood.
You Hart, had the bright front of the fall,
but we have the dull thud, and the pall
of it, all of it — you have at least the calm
of soul, rest in bosom, and we
no one or nothing to praise, no way to phrase
the shock of this strategy.

"SPIRITS ARE ORGANIZED MEN"

They are not fashioned with a weary look
at the dainty count of ten,
so it will be written in the iron book,
Atonatiuh knew
the meaning through and through.

Flag of ebony and oxbone whitened
in the sun, has been unfurled
because the ghosts of the sea have spoken
and your young-whitening hair floats upon
the swirling waters like ferns uncurled,
sea-faces, anemones, unaware of danger,
all these are token, sea-washed, sea-tossed token
that one we knew, with so much fenced
and parried through,
is never more to be else than a wild
wandering, sea-ranger—
fathom-filled, stalking somewhere in a chasm,
mild as a shepherd's child
or a blade of keel-grazing grass,
sailor, deck stranger, without compass.
And what is the iron purpose of it all,
to be pall-bearer and parson at one's own
funeral?
And none but sea-eyes peering ghoulishly in
through the slapping, trapping wave-din
windowed to excess, and no wall to stop
and give a neighbor-lover hope
hounded to the end, with wave-bend
and wave-trend.
Think of it, no green shutters more
to rattle, bang, unhang
themselves in a country-driven wind
no more pony-bridle's lilting silver tune
upon the air of Mixcoac, evening or noon,
all washed and thrashed away in seaslime
with maybe a sunken hulk for home;
What a cry, what a break, what a thunder
in a thought, and a hope come to naught,
what a whipping eye-dripping, blunder,

eye, heart, mind gone blind,
all of it, with the pall of it, asunder,
seatrapped by his own ill-timed device
slowly settling down a placeless precipice.
You could have done much better here, Hart—
facing of it, bracing to it, lacing with it.
There are vistas here that have their lon[e]liness,
arrogant hom[e]liness for spirits in distress,
there is every room for lofty lon[e]liness,
space for spirit's grace and spirit's restlessness.
We all know them and revere them—
there—is respite for a killing day or hour
avenues of blessedness to be thrilled to
when the dulled will resumes its effluence of power
as a flaming cloud comes over a savanna
of mortuary blue,
dispels the crucifixion of a moment or an hour
and makes the falsest false turn to true.
What does death to a body do, more
than send it further through the gates
where the end of end awaits,
and is not to be cheated, cajoled, outdone
where sun burns, or where is no sun.

And what will you do down there
hair and hands whitening to white,
teeth tightening, a spectacle for fright,
even to those used long since to scare
tremble, rock-rumble and moan?
It cannot give a sense to senselessness,
there are no birds there, no hands, no lips,
nothing but the lengthened out distress
of homelessness,
no laughter of the eyes or play of fingertips.
Why this harsh thrust of fierce opacity
nullifying finest gifts of clean translucency
all come to nought by the blackening of thought
with so much decent time spent clarifying time
to capriciously disconcert the rhyme.

"A TEAR IS AN INTELLECTUAL THING"

That well yourself had known, could know,
shed them copiously so, with no proud pondering
of why they came, or where they went,
products perfect of discernment.
Your eyes can have no tears, not now
but out of them will sprout and grow
branches of white quivering regret
for what they can no longer see, and loved to see;
what everlasting purgatory, not to see,
for to live by eyes alone is aspect
of eternal union, above the fro and fret,
above the last lost cry of the muezzin, shaken
from his parapet.

"THE WHOLE CREATION GROANS TO BE DELIVERED"

A beautiful dive, then floating
on his back, waved a hand,
and was seen, no more.

Over the bridge, the lengthless bridge
at last, as promised—
How could be, we believing the promising
when promising is all that men
have ever done, since there were men.
Who could believe that when
the clash and clang of noon had struck
down should go this one
to luckless luck
down to where the Jones' boys shake
a lively limb no more,
where, if eyes are open
as they sometimes are
in death, they cannot see
if star between them is,
as it so often was,
when every man seeks
semblance of his star.

Wash, wash, wash, so he will
and never again be still,
till nothing is left to wash,
or have swimmer's will.
Brother to the valleys and the hills
now, of what once were countries fresh and green
long since submerged in miles of water-sheen;
not a door, or a beckoning window-sill
not threshold of man to cross,
nothing but the toss, toss, toss
of writhing roof that shelter shall
no house.

Going, always going, till there is none
left to be gone, not a saving stone
for foot that cannot stand,
once so firmly set upon the land.
Wash brave then, to the last—
over the bridge, and bridge-end sunk
and not an eye to wink,
thanks to the sharks, short thoughts to think
whether it be right,
or downright erudite.

Return, return, never to return—
How say you are gone, when we
who had you know you to be,
know you to be near, in the sheer
now and ever, so long as sense
can keep a sense of pleasurable recompense.
How always is this clear
when near we know are near.

Broke boots and sides with wreaking laughter
just a day ago, and now the slow sure sweep
of indifferent deeps of deep
ship every laughter from its man-shaped laughter,
from its man-shaped rafter.
Well so it is, and the bridge-end broken
creaked from its moorings, and fallen in,
and all we can hear now is the din—

the last speech spoken,
promise kept, promise broken.

Gone to the end of the bridge and over
worn with roving the bridge, bridge-rover,
done with all the walking and the stalking,
and all the cheap talking.

AFTERLUDE

Voice from heartless vacuum
Points from out the winding cloak
and closet,
a long, long finger—IT IS DEATH,
IT IS DEATH, DEATH TO STAY, DEATH TO STAY,
DEATH TO STAY, OR GO AWAY,
IT IS DEATH ANYWAY.
You have heard this in your fuddled ears
like drip from a kitchen faucet
or a warning from Weybosset.

TANGENT DECISIONS (1935)

"How is it—I said to myself,
that I can possibly have lived
so long outside nature, without
identifying myself with her?
All things live, all things have
motion, all things correspond.
The majestic rays emanating from
myself to others, traverse without
obstacle, the infinite chain of
created things.
A transparent network covers the
world, whose loose threads communicate
more and more clearly with the planets
and the stars."

"I want to govern my dreams, instead
of endure them."

Gérard de Nerval

Stones to Wind

Be still
as we—
keep measure
of dream
thereby—
we have done service,
noble, geologic slavery—
service long,
patient,
honorable,
honored of life
and of death,

of living, of hour,
night, storm, suntime,
heard lisp of decades,
stuttering of centuries,
cheap impediment
of mantongue
clapper-hung—
clicking of woodchuck
teeth on root
of hurt heart—
loud boasting of thunder,
seismic innuendoes,
suncaked callings
of dark throat of love
weary of suncaked calling—
hitch-hike devotion,
multirushed commotion
gulped down in polished
lengths,
gushed trellis of crustacean
laughter, broken
with tidethrash
battalions of words
too sumptuously spoken.

■

Lapping of waters
thick, upon razorblade
selvages of sand,
pipers running on them,
wetting their shins
in the wave,
leaving little, lost signatures
of outmoded love,
patched, frayed, uncalled-for
love,
bauble bursting love,
dear inviolable thing—
for whom was right,
for whom was wrong,
devil-throng.

■

Hiccoughs of old ladies
who have sat on a porch
for their tithe of a
century,
old jewels cutting their
fingers,
have they given ear to pain,
learned death of spirit
from lean of bone?

130

■

why talk of cities
lit with cobra eyes,
to us, the rocks from Labrador
remarked, with vast
grey fortissimos
in their voices.
What have we to do
with dead places
like cities heaped
with dead faces,
glamour of dungeons
at dinner tables,
silence of bones in
cave more eloquent
than those slick fripperies
of repartee
behind enshrouded burgundy.

■

The mystic, kneeling
in the forests of Malines,
concocted words
made of skybreath
and golden tone,
columns to rely upon—
what else teach mystic
but skybreath and golden tone,
spirit union—
Perfect stillness,
Perfect fecundity—
spirit marriage here
contained,
wafer glowing
above bloodstream flowing.

■

Chitter of chipmunk
skipping on a wall of stones,
publishing plaint, towncrier
to the need of heartbroke mother
oriole.
Five infants, made of sunset
laughter,
plunged to death in niagara of wind—
five nuggets of gold from africas
in spring,
nothing to do but go into full
mourning.

■

West cheek to rose
of evening—feeling
its flesh burn with flush
of evening—
him beside himself
or calling up to himself
from far down below
in the hold of his own ship,
he, up in the rigging of his
former selves,
learning to straighten out
the tangle in the stiff
wind of evening.

Rose of evening.

You who are up there
in the rose of evening,
come down, leave me not
alone, among the rafters
and the joists of creaking
custom,
take me up with you into
the rose of evening,
plant my lips to the rose of
evening—

Man talking to himself
in the rosa mystica
of evening.

Signatures of Multiple Things

Signatures,
written down in careless hand
on parchments of indifference;
procession of bird's feet
on windrushed sands that have
lost their way among pebbles,
unwanted pebbles, and
split flays of shells.

Coat of a man
of the sea —
darkblue, left flattened
on smoketone weeds,
swerved patterns of salt
flecking them —
as if owner had slipped out of it
in a hurry, disturbing
neither warp nor woof.

Brown bird,
twoblade knife
of brown,
cutting into reams
of wind —
signatures of multiple
things.

You walk among the
little bits of things
the sea has washed back —
troubled beings come, and say to
the sea, take these things, I have
had enough of them, and they give
the sea these things, to take —
where?
she brings them back, lays them
all together, and you find yourself
walking among many things that have
troubled men and women —
why does the sea bring them back?

Curved, pale fancies
rounded with unspokenness
of many beings caught in nets,
held there in heaps,
fish when net is drawn in,
gasping for their several
elements,
oblique lamentations of
unpainted women are with
them.

So many sizes, so many hues,
sea saying to itself, why all
these signatures of multiple
things, behaviours out of tune,
mouchoirs of remorse,
curved locks of vacant hair,
lisped vagaries, monstrous deceits,
blatant deaths of outlawed epithets,
stonecold laughter from high
positions,
despair of cooks at fallen recipes,
last, lost vanities of given-up
amours,
struggle of monogram on heraldry
to regain its owner, or vice versa
of it,
revolt of wooden indian at paper gate,
vain reproach from picket fence
toward ivies without inclination
to lean.

A woman's coat, tossed
to sea,
wrap of servant at dismissal,
coat of woman who waited too long
and with fevers of disgust
threw servile coat at nature,
All these have paid their tithe
"of mint, anise, and cinnamon"—

Inscribing

Signatures of multiple
things.

Hollander's Animal Faith

I saw a shadow on a jut of stone
for it was middle afternoon,
Hollander all made of that,
singing his magnificat—
I to flesh and bone
all sunk in mats of oozy weed
meshed and plaited
on stout rocks on which an owl
from north had lately sat—
plaited like beard on heaving
triton's chest,
pressed forward to a burning
west.
Sun was coppering all of it
along the whole sea wall of it.

Shadow of this man came down
shot along my shoulders brown
of width that only triton['s] own
was shadow,
leaving wrap of friendly sense
around,
as sky would cleave ground.

The[n] came the ruddy face and brow,
hands, arms, and thighs done now
in same thick summer tone—
his smile was also like the dip
of middle afternoon;
"We'll not be sorry for this day"—
with this he leapt from stone to stone
in goat-way, fearlessly,
let fall his loose, scant garb,
his manness out to every wind—
majesty of earth was wound
about his tense smooth frame,
he seemed about to break, almost
for sense of nature's clarity.
Knowing not what else to do
he sang aloud, and a thin, clear

evening bell came from his metal throat
he being thoroughly in love
with this, or that,
or, so he thought.

"I wouldn't take many dollars
for this day,"
said Hollander to me in moment
of delay
between earth joy and seaspring,
"just let it be this way
till end of end, and I'll not ask
for any other thing."
He seemed more, man-made into Man
as sometimes rougher humans can.

"I will take it as it is,
let no one try to make it else
or other,
let no one waste a human bother—
I'll have it as I find it,
dear, mellifluous, and kind
morning, noon, and night,
for I am blind with love,
there's nothing else to prove."
A woman danced before his eyes,
burning with terrific strategies,
each had been dealt an early blow
but found that love is ever new.
Nothing else to prove but love—
said Hollander—love gives the shape
and size of everything,
"I'd rather be in love, than king."
Plain tale enough, as old as width or place,
the sun-hued lustre on his face
spoke extasy of illimitable space—
he dashed from rock to thrashing sea
with seaman mastery.

Sestets

Swirls of brown, dark, swaying
on leaping flank of sky—thirsting,
so they seemed, for some oblique oratory
or, was it merely, plain width of
common silence yearned for,
somewhere to be—bird-at-home.

Wedges of black wings, incising
triangles toward some digit of the south—
what hurries them, harries them, gives them cue
from impresario of seasons, this the last triumphant
escapade
have they taken tip, for orient's spectacular?

None knew what pinned huddling
gulls together among reeds of tawn,
seared with oriole blood
of spendthrift autumn afternoons
pointed to windward like caporals riveted
to command—you should have seen them pointing.

Did ever legendary hoof skip over
tips of these reeds, as this wind
in high speed velocities of October,
wingwhipped to missions, to fly fast,
make good go of it, bring back in
return, news of freezing frontier?

Lashed to mast of their parti-coloured decisions
sitting on one side, as a top, in pool of indecisions
as if dry cloth could ever live
in press of cirrus, drop by drop,
drop by drop, through any certain summer
day, nothing to do but let them.

Over marshes heard, white voice
of salt yearning from it, comes yellow sound,
earth playing marches to itself in marshes,
singular opportune waving of firebrand
effusion suffices
coming as it does from tangle of woodbine,
along those rubicund clusters of sumac.

Miracle Cary, and His Twelve Loaves—Twelve Fishes

Miracle Cary, anchorite of sense
with wild, hopeless disregard
of recompense,
held out his hands, all gloved
with mercy to the crowd,
shed smiles that winged their
kindly way to tired selvages
of worn, tattered men, frayed
with callousness of winter,
with diffidence of summer flayed,
saying softly to them as nurse
would say to sick one in a bed,
you who have been clutched with hunger
kissed with eager mouth of death,
leering, loveless pain-monger
who eats man's breath
as he walks,
you who have known
the lush, full nourishment
of stone,
come close,
I have fishes and rich width
of bread,
given me by the longsuffering dead,
who cannot hear the cry of men alone
without some deed be done,
or thin word said—
come close, brothers of me,
I have tithes of loaves and fishes
for you.

Miracle Cary
is a flophouse saint
or something equally true and quaint,
with soft, intriguing tenderness
of heart,
if ever he frowns it must be
within,
for smile is all one ever sees
on Cary's face, or broad Irish grin—

141

You never can do a thing for Cary
for he has too much to do for you.
A poor man asked him
to a plate of meat,
Say—said Cary, you come to
my place and eat,
I got a kettle of soup,
real stuff in it,
good bone, carrots, beans
and other worthy earthly things,
just out of earth, sweet, fragrant,
full of their own worth—
I make it once a week and eat
it till it's gone.
And somehow it is his look
has won.

Turning to me—says Cary
who is always busy
with a heart for beaten men,
he being one—he knows his men—
I never can take anything
from them—I'd rather give
them something,
and he looked far out to sea
while his throat grew heavy
with mercy.

You know those men that downwent
to the sea,
standing there, weightfooted, looking
upward toward the upwardly,
'Twas them that sent me fish, and ravens
brought me bread,
so Cary said—
I have an awful need,
said Cary to the earth,
these men have been empty
from birth,
I have to feed them, they belong
to me, looking somewhat like saint

in muffled quandary.
This is not an old man's job,
said Miracle, flushed
with youth's own pride.
It's something for the young to do
who know
whip of hunger in wind
learning early to be kind—
You get soft with a life like this
and your heart gets to be twice as
big as it is,
with all these flophouse miseries,
pain brings this kind of men together,
if only to learn from each other
the thin tense comedies of pain
over again.

Cary put his pennies
on a good man's eyes,
to keep them from the shining sun,
I was glad I could do that much
for the good man gone.
Cary will get wings one day
if there's a place where such
things be.

Sea Engraving—Style of 1880

You will drive out over edges
of marshes at ebb or flow of tide,
there will be gulls sitting, white,
grey against dark banks that fold under
like blankets on a bed—they will
seem to be sitting in brown fields
for the backwashes of the sea are low
under them.

Sometimes you may see also, up to his
knees in mud, the clamdigger—for these
back washes are fine for seeding and feeding;
Autumn will enhance all this by her rich
ravishment.
You will come to a width of dune, and
suddenly, like a veil lifted on some scene
for monologues celestial,
the line of swishing waters dividing
here from there, you from earth you have just
walked on, from what, as you look out to sea,
might seem like, suddenly, passages from the
book of Thel to be opened on the sky,
and spoken.
It comes like a shock almost, this scene, it will
enter that archaic space called the center
of you—give it twinge, as if—now I know I can say it—
here is the place where all things can be said
and touch no one, can have it out with the thing
that nature says is her in you and you in her.
Starfish loses its star here, the gentle lapping of
waters loosens the tramp of birdsfeet and they float
away like little white things hurrying to find
their lost imaginings—it puts to the test here
the so common courage of love—and in moment of
super-praise you could be wanting to say, can God
be a place, or a look, or a line—if this is God's
face then how truly handsome he is.

Unshackled, bodyfree-spirit-sense-meaning of time-

144

space-atom-"mystery of Opening" indeed be this,
augustinian gateway to perfection.

"I was directed to accept your invitation by
obedience to the spirit"—
"Friends are born on archaic horizons,
they were shaped with the Pteraspis of
Siluria—they have nothing to do with the
accidents of space"—
or some of those sober pious sonnets of Jones
Very must have been born here;

I want to look like this place looks, I want
to be a piece of it and its looks, live inside
of its looks.

All things could be settled here—all things
following this white line could be settled
for eternity.

"Nature has no outline, but imagination has;
Nature has not tune, but imagination has";

And when the lady saw the place she said,
O how like Nordeney it is, so like Nordeney—
and this word too seemed to be something
like its name.

OCTOBER AFTERNOON

October Afternoon

These dulcet euphonies of autumn now begun
flecking the pathway of the gull and the heron
white sweep and blue sweep through this
northern canyon
of granite where fir hemlock spruce and pine
invoke the freedom of their settled plane
crowding the eye with exclusive eclectic strategy
walking through the fernstrewn aisles
after leaving the little settlement of Bluecheek
sitting by the road
noting their ceremonious paperwhite smiles
bonehued now remembering October
bone that still breathes speaking a language
of its own
fungushued too tinged with fungus liv[e]liness
of tone
pallor possibly of someone living loving
someone dead
along the selvages of this still desultory stream
that since there is no skyflood cannot feel
itself flow and so
bears its share of chromatic ration
worthy of its menial station
and the look of philatelic variation
smearing the mouldhued surface
its blue-imbued ruminating face
flicked glories fallen from special pockets
undelivered letters lying loose for want
of proper address—no such person—not here—
and they go back to where they came from
with ingratiating smile
returning to the department of casual insignificant
affairs

these ornate tables of the registering earth
crowded with inquisitional extravagances
for state occasions admirably arranged
now fed from by bevies of brown birds—
birds who break chromatic breads
with their invisible lords
and who exactly is "Seigneur" among the birds
and if the partridge at this season grace
does say
what thankfulness shall he alone convey.

■

Two grey herons flying
from white bridge—outward
into the mist where the river
meets the sea—gives into it
marks like two slow-gliding arrows
the way the evening falls;
images of departure
way of all things, clear
into the wide fields
the exquisite areas of memory.

■

these exquisite mementos
of the generations
passing across the light
at the end of summer—
sliver
of living grey hair
look of one suffering
on the edge of fields
those flute-tones in the
smiles of the young
proud splendour of
things that know their
end will one day come
prepared to face
their quiet
devastations.

the fish-hawk, making
a left turn suddenly,
as he sees the belly of the fish
swerve upward
to the early sun—
closing of eye of robin
who told of untoward fate
seared forehead of simple boy
who knows too well his life will
never begin,
he will see it through the blinding
dust of other behaviours
simple one—be patient
perhaps there will come to you, too—
memento of the generations.

Go Lightly

Evening moth
sips at mouth
of some flowers,
his feet touching
spirit-like
their lips—
go lightly, said moth
to himself
for delicate is honey
of the evening.

morning is filled
with humming;
if you put your ear
to the telegraph pole
you can hear the world
saying bon jour
to the world.

this mysticism
of the antennae
reaching out, as tendrils
of the vine
bringing certain laughters
to the troubled
soul.

To H. C.

Seeing it first, eye filled with
certain certitudes
the brightened lustre of plain moods
come nacreous
to recompense us.

The day revealing its own marvel
to our consecutive ear
evening blended in chromatic treasuries
in a theme, won
from secular emotion.

Hand to hand
bringing heart to itself
to seize the contraband,
nothing quite said
nothing done or undone
yet the moment, finespun.

■

it is as if at times
one can hear the darkness
talking to itself—talking
to itself—to itself, talking.

I open my door in
the evening—
I look out of it, and save
for the reflection of the lamp
on the ashboughs above, through
the window,
I would say—there is nothing,
yet it must be the darkness
talking to itself.

suddenly there is a light
reddish rather than whitish
and I know it is the hermit
woman,
coming to feed the teacher's cats.

■

how like the sea
to be
always certain
of its lyric fluency.

often it is
like this
with terrible mysteries.

stiff tone of death
in every wave
what more can wave have
save perhaps a little love
or the look of something
only flowers leave
when they pass,
precise curve,
soft breath.

islands wait
with certain consternation
fixed, immediate contemplation—
it is its exact reward
to live unheard
of continent.

Invitation

Some take their walks at night
and that's exciting
you see the lovely world at its best
when it is fighting
in the act of making love
without the prettiness of plighting—
raw love just off the spit
such are accustomed to it.

Some take their walks in the morning
and they are probably religious
like the primitives who feel
that dawn is something to be worshipped
like the indian the growing of his corn
like h[im]—they ask it to be gracious
and come to something more
the morning comes to noon in time
but they have had the spirit's prime.

If I say it's after noon for me
it might seem tritely snobbish
but I like to see what I can see
and like it when the worst is over
there is something comes upon the day
that has nothing to do with dew and
clover—
I like the loud repeat of after noon
when all the voices that I want to hear
are clarion
in their tone.
I like the colour and the hue
of all this afternoon fanfare
if that is snobbish,
then I am one.

Pray pick your time, erratic person
and what you get will be your own.

■

Yesterday, in the night
summer died;
we heard it in the creaking
of the doors and window frames
there was a strange drunkenness
in the air
before the morning broke.

arriving at the portal
of the morning—I looked out
of the window to the tidal river,
what did my eyes behold—
death of summer.

I could tell the way the gulls
faced the north wind
they were paid mourners
for the obsequies of the dead
with folded wings—here and there
a cry of recognition, to the north.

summer had died beautifully,
said one of them—
others merely laughed in the manner
of the children of the sea.

what is one summer—the dark one said,
the sea has buried hundreds of them
and they folded their wings more firmly
for they feared the common eulogy
that follows casual affairs.

Pot-Luck among the Casuals

A dog came loping to his side
have you any of a speechless bone
no—but I have foul weathers in
my head,
and why should you want another one
you who are all but wrack of bone
and nearly dead,
why—very wind plays tunes upon
your ribs—the birds could build a nest
in the hollow of your spine
who is it fed you on broken stone
you walking, pallid skeleton?

he gave him hunk of what he had
'tis good enough for me—none, or so he said,
when you want to go, is sweeter—
from worse to something better;
bone will maybe sharpen teeth
but makes pain sharper underneath—
a bowl of downright summer blood
would do you heaps of good.

the dog looked up to him and said,
save me—save me from a speedy grave
give anything of what you have;
he gave two hunks of what he little had
it was as if his jaw would crack
it felt so good—
a smile came out of canine face
and fairly shamed the listless place—
a dog that wants, is tragical to see—
we're used to men that get that way.

LAUGHTER OF STEEL

Laughter of Steel   1

The laughter of steel
is a nifty laugh
first it signs a simple
contact
then, a simple epitaph.

wouldn't you think it
would just get sick
of being its mortuary self
so costly, so murderously
slick.

You see them in the photograph-
ics of the magazines on life,
the men caress the shells like
newborn babe
with everything to forgive
wandering in a cherry grove.
They are oiled and duly kept
in the very pink of condition
commensurable with their sancti-
monious station.

The shells—they call them very
reverently
and certainly it is very plain to see
they are meant for a most fictitious
majesty.

Laughter of Steel 2

There is a vicious laughter of
steel
in every shining projectile.
It is not satisfied until
it sees a hole in every heart
a surfeit of ache and smart
beneath a roof and in a gleaming
eye—
Death is but the filth of some foul
yesterday
who is cheaply brave, has not time
to cry;
the sun shines decently on every curve
of steel
and does not ask if it be good or bad
to shine on steel,
it is statistically dumb to pain,
each morrow has the same refrain
and history is old baggage, then.

Pistols for Pleasure—Guitars for Defense

They sing in the darkness
of the ravishment of love
and of its emptiness
tightening their bullet-filled belts
so that their breathing will be
less friendly—
see them standing in dark doorways
all the way from the Alameda to the
Molino Verde
smiling with corn-stiffened teeth
as if at the sulphurblue moonlight—
it is hatred that is beautiful to them
not love—
love is for release
hatred for satisfaction—
black is the beauty among the
bullets,
the plucked guitars yield nothing
but the empty sound of love
and the vast danger of this
honesty.

A Present to the Sun

They killed him, just to really see
if his child's thoughts were worth
a shining penny—
corrosion killed the lustre of
his iridescent youth
and something stilled his mouth
from telling pauper truth.

He thought it was something very great
when off he far too glowing went
to keep an odious, ill-smelling sacrament—
the mothers gave their flesh and bone
so tellingly
as flowers on a bright spring day
at the passing of a president—
they wore their specious stars of gold
to keep from growing cold.
It was all so pompously poetical
until a something big became so small
the children cannot see their way
to flaming glory
and this—the gist of many a story.

(1) *Marsden Hartley, aged about five.* (Marsden Hartley Memorial Collection, Treat Gallery, Bates College, Lewiston, Maine.)

(2) *Marsden Hartley on the banks of the Androscoggin River, Maine, ca. 1910.* (Marsden Hartley Memorial Collection, Treat Gallery, Bates, College, Lewiston, Maine.)

(3) *Portrait bust of Marsden Hartley by his friend Arnold Rönnebeck, bronze, Paris 1912. (Whereabouts unknown.)* (Photo courtesy of Leon Tebbetts, Hallowell, Maine.)

(4) *Marsden Hartley in Berlin, 1922.* (Marsden Hartley Memorial Collection, Treat Gallery, Bates College, Lewiston, Maine.)

(5) The New York Times *clipping showing Marsden Hartley (left) with Ezra Pound (center) and painter Fernand Léger at the Café du Dôme, Paris, 1926.*

(6) *Marsden Hartley, ca. 1923.* (Courtesy Sylvia Beach Collection, Princeton University.)

(7) *Marsden Hartley, ca. 1923.* (Courtesy Sylvia Beach Collection, Princeton University.)

(8&9) *Two photographs acquired by Marsden Hartley of fragments of Egyptian sculpture at the Metropolitan Museum of Art in New York, from which he wrote the three poems (pp. 179–181). Left, gray marble face of King Amenemhat III, Bequest of Mrs. H. O. Havemeyer, 1929. Right, fragment of a head of a statue which, in 1927 was labelled "Head of Queen Nefertiti," Purchase, Edward S. Harkness Gift, 1926, from the Carnarvon Collection.* (Hartley's copies of these photographs are in the Memorial Collection, Treat Gallery, Bates College, Lewiston, Maine.)

Soldier on His Knees in the Snow

Hail Mary—Mother of everything
that is perfectly true
I would sing a soldier's song to you.
When I came in to this frigid place
the heart of it so dark—the eye
of it like you—the eye of it like you
sky being eye of the place
in which you are
Mary Mother.

I saw the hem of your gracious dress
through every branch—on every childish lip
for even snow throws quietly up
lights from the pale bosom of your
dress,
and I yearned for your deep, enfolding
caress,
Mary Mother.

My beads are white as the tears of
children in their ten dreams lost
shivering at the ashen cost
of their nacreous themes
of being merely human—
no man can ever be a man
in snow upon his knees
he is a child craving Motherly caresses
it is the world he looks at makes
him bow his head
to pray to Mary Mother for the living
more—than for the dead.

Light-Heavy at Prayer

Punching the bag, running to the basket
praying to Mary and Joseph and Francis,
or even Thomas d'Acquin maybe
to explicate theology
skipping rope on a cake of ice
because
it is good to be calm at all times
especially in the ring.

Hail Mary full of grace,
now step as light as a feather over
the rope,
tap it-tap it-tap it—Hail Mary
blessed art Thou—blessed is—
be sure you hit the bag in the right place
not on the side where the punch will
glance off—

Hail Mary
blessed art thou—Hail Mary.

And the wind blew across the desert
of his loneliness—his thoughts fluttering
like flower dust back to Madawaska
all the time
and down some little river back in Acadia
some little river of June—
all youth is some little river of June,
the seeds coming up on its banks
throwing out young shoots so much earlier
than expected
bulbs springing to fresh green
and the orioles high in the swinging elms
knitting a swing basket out of anything
that will weave comfortably.

Where else does life lie for such as this
who keeps sanctuary in his soul
at seven forty-five every morning
among the candles and the bleeding

hearts.
O Mary Mother—make me good inside the
ring,
give me a fair decision.

Boston Common — Long Time Ago

It is long now I met a man
well, he was neither man or woman
being deathly sick at heart
suffering from a world old smart
the tulips were swinging quietly
like all the minor bells of spring
the wooden swans on the lake were thinking
as only wooden swans would dare to do,
not me — or you.

The thing called life had shown him out
and shut the gate —
plenty room outside it said
then drew the squeaking bolt
without a trace of etiquette.
He came to me as if he thought me
human
saying — may I look into your blue eyes
I am not asking for anything, you see
and cold winds blew across his aching lip.

Your eyes — they make me think of Mother
Mary's robes when she is walking in the
garden
her huge day's work done —
Never mind, look all you want to
I said — I said
I couldn't know I had what he
most needed;
then through the rivers of salt he
smiled
and — thank you sir — he said — goodbye.
It was myself who lived another vast
oblique simplicity.

OBLIQUE FRONTIER

This Living in Small Place

When the flood of gelid extasy has done
its frayed mechanics turn
and the hulk lies on the reef languidly
or stretch of shore, because nothing
wants it off, letting it lie
to take up room only its cold vertebrae could crave,
and all the deaths of little longings line
the pierced fatuous horizon
like cursed curvatures of shells,
and the day all laughter hustled to its doom
is written on each scarp and cliff
as on the lintel of some blasted tomb
and the much expected dove will not resume
its honied hieroglyph
where broken dreams have festered
and dropped their skypressed folds
like petals on a brace of wind
and there is no matching of beloved scenery
with lengths of emblazoned radiancy
where even dogs go blind
and must be conducted to their
accustomed offices,
and women have the worst of it too, who
being brave, choose effigies to be at home with,
the report of how the heron as it flies, toes in,
the curve of its neck like a flattened S
and there is semblance of mismanaged business
in every creak of spine.

Watching

Watching winter drop its white punctuations
upon the city of many finished paragraphs and
phrases as if saying—there are so many
sentences finished and done with, so many sentences—
periods must be dropped into place—
the sky seeming half weeping half thinking
with its many white punctuations, the many paragraphs
to do with them.
Sometimes it is "I love you" in desperate need
of a period.
Sometimes—"could it not have been otherwise"
"I will do all you wish and say nothing"
"What a day it must be in the quiet end of
the country"
"Is there no cure for all this protracted insomnia"
"Must flowers wither and fall from the stalk
without blessing someone"
these—and the so many other phrases
in search of the white punctuation
of winter.

Oblique Frontier

When the seaswell takes me in
at the scattering
shaking its saltness over my disheveled
shaking
bone,
and the sharpest wave tries to drown out
the last all but lost note in my throat
that is that was—for being silenced now
and compatibly still like stone
therefore beyond brute shout
the wind protesting impecunious will
and cannot shoulder
or make heart bolder
to bear the power of the word one
instant longer
that word shall make itself free
of profligate mystery
and help me somehow to outcry
thanks for this immitigable parity
my choked whisper shall have empirically then
been made clarion
flag flung up to stave
nonsense of the grave
or, dual faced oblivion.

Perhaps Macabre

Thank heaven there are trees that bare—
we like our skeleton with sky
interlacing the wrack
and when the leaves are hyperthick
it sort of makes us sick
yet we perhaps know why.

We have to go through so much
that's covered,
but when the strutting trees are bared,
and we see each agued bone clutch
at areas of azulite,
it makes us feel we can sit tight
and not be bothered.

I know everything about that shell—
you do, I said—it must be very hard
to know an all that well,
don't you see it makes one so responsible
and think of knowing any all too soon
we must eat gravel with a pewter spoon
ponder that, and manage if you can,
it will help your folding skeleton.

She thinks the bone is prettiest
when riveted to sky
it helps her we assume to brave
a certain majesty
and kills the click of monotone;
that's me, she often softly said
as if only perfect thing is whispered
pointing to a wrack of bone with roses on
its floating jib, and the teeth gone
on its own airness doting.

O—carve away the rancid flesh
and let us see the ample skeleton—
she lets no tear fall from a socket
but takes a digit for her locket
and wraps it in a mesh of snow-

blown leaves brought her from a crater's lip
all cluttered up in frothy white
she loves her sleep.
With thou, I never shall be lonely
or know blast of melancholy.

Perhaps macabre?

I give her to you as she mainly was
she with the snow-white stone shut jaws
she loved the smell of voiceless chalk
and the rattle of her own talk
it staved the breath of evening off
and gave her suppertime to scoff.

Trapezist's Despair

This over-sensuous trapezist
mistaking the butterflies upon the silk
of his garments for symbols of preened satisfaction,
of mannish laughter, or even of acrobatic vanity—
and who, flying like this very winged thread into the
warp of oblique tenacity and of hourly death across the
emblazoned garden, which, when it was young, had not ear for
minutes' miseries:—
Who could have for a moment thought that under this
very set of wings
there burned the battered centaur upon a raging hill,
all shot with spears from heaven-attack, shivering as he
writhed with pitiable revenge, pawing the dust in anguish,
this rapacious trapezist, finding himself
at the dead end of love, shoots his pretty partner, saying
"I guess this is the last thing I can do for you, Vera"
and with that, does himself in, also.
Alfredo, the sparkling-upon-the-air—
all the bones are broken now, and the bright
scintillating wisps of glittered memory, tattered into
floating ribbons moaning for the sun,
and Lalo—left alone
to make of it, what—but the best he can:—
and the little Lillian starkest shape in heaven,
crying down,
Afredo, what have you done,
what have you done, Alfredo?

He Too Wore a Butterfly

He wore a butterfly upon his flanks,
upsetting the woman and the ship in their angles,
and down his midrib the image of Christ, the feet
and the nails, touching his navel.
He wore a butterfly upon his shoulder blade and
one above his knee, as if—like the indian in the
race, whose thighs are brushed with eagle feathers to
give him speed in the run.
He wore a butterfly upon his flanks as though he
felt the fear of being musclebound,
or, saying to himself—"I must have the breath of
spring upon my beam"—that smiling morning of a man
and—as if the sea had crowded all its waves
within his eyes, making him think of numberless
casual afternoons, the lashes curling up to let the
floods of evening in,
staving off for later years the pale textures of
immitigable distance.

For Gaston Lachaise — a Sort of Written Frieze

As if by some fault divine, creating an
extra note in the seven reed syrinx
most, as we heard it in the streets of
Paris
the blue hair of the shepherd
hanging down under his hat in pressed
coils as grapes pressed under the winepress
where the feet do the pressing with
voluptuous laughter
as if to get the last sacred drops from
the hills
ere life went out of them, supinely —
the goats climbing the angular escaliers
as they are wont to do,
          the young dreamer in the Cluny praying
perhaps at some gothic rosace
the gleam of the impeccable Chartres shot
back through it — causing this pagan
the sought for pain
this blood leaping back over the hills again
in the fashion of the great beautiful animal
of the much forsaken flesh — lying down
then to drunken sleep once more,
and
waking
eyes burning hot as doors of furnaces
when opened to show flame is there —
out over the edges of these dumbfounded lids
blinking at their unbelievable discoveries
smoke flames and convulsive lavas
rising flowing descending upon courageous
vestiges of night
despising its own silences patricianly
the huge torches of atomic revelry
flaming up against his cherished cliffs
all feathery with obsidian ferns weaving
already meshes of inviolable attraction
and the vast faun being led by the forelock
with his forest tangled hocks to feed thereafter
forever

upon roots where very bark is bread
until the great clock slew him with
its far tempestuous hour, beating
heraldic victories upon his anvil
breast.

For the Shut Eye

of the wholesome, lonesome ones
who, because they do not develop as
vines envelop a wall, climbing over the
stones, the bricks, the mortar, the barbed
appendages which announce cruelty at the top
to prevent sins of a kind that are a menace
to mankind,
namely—not seeing because the shut eye
will not see because it cannot see, if it is
not opened widely, largely, roundly, willingly
without premonition, prejudice, or canting
philosophical jargon, attached to its gills
through which it breathes.
Nothing will let the shut eye open if there
is not willingness to escape from the eye being
shut, and no ordinance from the police
will make this possible—
it must all come from willingness to
openness, and a natural desire to escape
what is sometimes known under the name of
STUPIDITY.
The shut eye must not be incriminated
of this too heavily, since it is bound to stay
behind its lids that are closed doors
to the gateway of orient miracle, and
all but countless of these nights that make
day love, and a going forth to the quaint
engendering paradise.

NEW RAINS WASH DOWN

Soliloquy in Dogtown, Cape Ann

To have come among you, rocks—
not with woodchuck's foraging insolence
where levity of dust so anciently has blown
giving certain lengths and widths of plain renown
where junipers stand thick beside you, and
themselves,
making organpipes for fugues and fierce
recessionals of wind that parry and pierce
the flesh and bone of mortal mind
left to suffer its own windblown oblivion.
Bayberry sprays are spread like cloaks
above the shapes of much-forgotten folks—
cellars do not hide or ghost or shape
but their own effigy in dusky, musky escape
between the flourishing of hurried seeds
to fleet the gluttony of blustery, purposeless
weeds.
Come among you rocks then, solemnly, and speak
not even to the wings that pass in flurry
to encompass earth and sea, and other windwing
worry.
I sit a spell, clutching at plain thoughts, wrenching at
no secrecies, hearing the magnificat
of afternoons and mornings united in their theme
but broken up in segments by the bought
extravagances of dream, wrenched and torn,
warped and twisted, whisperings of the forlorn
deceptive moment they were born—
I sit, and note the stiff obliqueness of the north
that mothers ever strangling mirth of you
glance desultorily among you as might an albatross
if it would descend to such an instant's levity
marking pontifical simplicity ranging over all

your means and ways of being dutiful and proud
ignoring every menace of lightning shaft or cloud
that clutches enmity within its fists, or trysts
with thunder at the mouth of death
terribly suspending the breath.
I hear the fugues and recitatives swell out,
then die out
in whispers of emaciated wind, suppressing shout
or cry or what suppressed emotions answer by
and nothing seems to tell of high impress
or infidel redress. It is a place up here
where, confess, converse, sphere and sphere,
detect, rehearse, delete, and in the last complete
their everlasting trend, world without end,
fast or slow,
the way they always know and go,
officials to the omnivorous
paraclete.

Alice Miriam

Speak—Alice
speak
from out the wastes
of myth and mystery
from whence no word
has ever come—
and do they give you music
for a meal,
and harmony for home?

Is there light upon your street
and when you strangers meet
must you too commiserate?
It must then be just as dumb
as this earth's pandemonium.

I see you clad in drear
imperishable snow
and would not have it so.
I think it is your laughter
that I sometimes hear
ringing gently like no other
laughter in my ear—
I see a light from out your
prismical blue eye
go straight across my visage
as I pass
the effigy that once was
you—
how like it seems
the life that once I knew
when you were not shelved
among celestial dreams.

Geometric Death

Six leaves there are of these
curled, twisted, whirled upon a stem,
fluted,
sombrely convoluted
as if to conjure among the six
perfect confirmation of brown death
to fix
from which no leaf can falter
no lease conviction alter,
no shifting breath or heaving wind
shall change, remove, uncurl, or stir
out of communal trust, united erudition
of one fabric with eternal mind.
Exquisite mummies are these leaves
coiled in their own perfume as sheaves
of grain are redolent of their last breath
against the stipulation of this regal
spirit
who weaves a glistening winding sheet
and draws the season's life within it—
a noble geometric falls, majestically
determined.

King Amenemhat III

If a little bit of useless stone
morsel of earth—sinew and bone
find use above itself to here
regard a man's significance so clear
King Amenemhat,
I wish that fate
had spared the rest of you intact,
your visage is so perfect.
A mask that hides no masculine desire
and still maintains its poise
by touch of cosmic fire
exudes a gentleness extreme
and wears nobility of peace
as regally as queen her diadem—
I think all Egypt must then
have held to one consent,
for you are magnificent.
The perfect thing we have been told
by estheticians bold
is perfected in all its parts,
peculiar province of the arts—
this perfect being your delicious mask
is all that beauty-loving sense
could ask
for recompense.
All men should look on you
with man's discerning eye
and note their own discrepancy.

Queen Nefertiti—Small Fragment of Nose and Mouth Only
(Canarvon Collection, Metropolitan Museum)

Behind these pulsing lips
of feminine voluptuary,
what sanctuary
of birth and death
of sudden lusts grown warm
then cold,
silent with their loss of breath
beneath
these planetary curves
where finger-tip reserves
the right to cherish
that from which it perish.
How can a stone
give forth so much of amatory breath
and still be living its own ageless death
or nostril in the flesh
quivering with life—enmesh
more nuance of amatory bliss
than this?
If faces had what little stone
can give, beneath their hopeless bone
we'd say
with unalloyed alacrity,
how splendid to behave that way.
Alas, for human frailty,
it cannot keep
what stone has kept from sleep.
How dead the faces seem
that look at you,
who cannot believe you to be true.

Same Fragment — Second Look

If a moment out of voiceless history
surely the greatest in the given dynasty
recovered from the maws of wanton
and promiscuous death
with such velocity
in stone —
breathe human breath
from out its perfect plane, this amatory plane
more human
than a million replicas of living travesties
can give,
what must a night among the whispering wings
that hover on your lips have known,
statistical with fiercely swift imaginings?

O, mouth inevitably made for craving
because it moves and moves
without a trace of conciliatory saving
atom of illimitable loves
because it needs must give and give
to live.
Do lips like yours lack ever the experience
or lure of simple innocence?

It is the brave conceit
in lieu of his immitigable defeat
who senses,
to yearn for further recompenses
than this stone can state —
it is huge aspect of the inarticulate.

Modigliani's Death Mask

Amedeo—
How can death be beautiful
as you are in the tender clutch of death?
Ask one who suffered him to come early,
heart, soul, body-bloom dissevered
if death be beautiful—
on his cooled lips the single last smile
of a young nun, at the first faint glimpse
of all-revealing Paradise,
cool in the snowy glamour of death,
without hunger of heart, anguish of bone
tremor of the soul, no more.
Is it here you dream now
Amedeo,
in dream, white with ardour of sky-blossoming,
no more cheap earth-tossing, and splendour-throe
of love for transitory perfectness—
and we who sit mildly, equivocally by
in spite of all longing to be free,
where we, living in that world of special knowledge
special ignorance, intuitive delight,
in silence of despair,
touched almost to respectable tears,
as deep thoughts often are by the smile
of such a man with the sad, high-broken heart,
death's inviolable decision by death's own self
spoken,
O beauteous face, Amedeo, made perfecter with peace,
Let not death or hate remove the sweet placidity,
keep death, this tryst with loveliness,
in Mitla keep this tryst.

Fence Between

Let not in—difference
keep pact of this sin, in no sense—
how other shade or tithe of new degree
become for us a wheezed perplexity
who have for all, once for all
the stalwart, magnificent whole.
We who had it first, have it ever now—
there is not change upon this changeless brow.
Why give up a faultless, haltless prow
to smoothing hands on shiftless steering
wheel
which has no heart of warm, endearing
steel.
Fence, pray, and what, where, how?
Can come, no such implied, imperious modicum
to us who say, and seeing soon
our never lost, never won, our boon,
kept holy to the different day,
aloof from all this froward fancy play—
the thing, still one for two, and two for
one,
then one and one and one be ever three—
trinity of north with blossoms
at the finger's ends,
triangular recourse so ordered long before
holds union with which opaque uniqueness blends
and makes translucent, to take in floods
of orienting sun
giving us all in all of one
and one, and one.

New Morning—and the Years Are Ours

To an all-time, now-time, no-time
yet-time eminence of theme
trisectory dissension of a spoken day
the fourth will matter not, spoken or broken
to our plausible display of year or yearful love
accustomed as we are to dovewing move
of every touch and go, pretty showdown
long since built of huge renown;
for only three at least, and we the three
what cause for spacious jealousy.
New morning, and the years are ours
we who brought them thickness of interwoven
flowers,
and laid the business up above dark showers,
to heighten three-toned, three-timed stout
affections' crown.

M. T. — a Relative in Certain Aspects of Metaphysical Divination

To you, so affluently mystical
at times,
almost jesuitical
in moments of defense
seeking as it were
astrological rhymes
to stress the atoms
of your sense
of logical existence,
warmed with spectrum-hues
of sudden birth
and almost desperate clarity
to encompass inevitable disparity,
pulsing with the breath
of living faith
that only martyrs in belief
can suffer
then turning pallid with the hue
of death,
as if to be engulfed in human love
once it is revealed
were not permissible
when documents are duly signed
and sealed.

How empty all desire for self
you say — or seem to say
distressing any hosts that bless
with calm humility
to seek forever that integral degree
consistent with a given continuity
spirally
above this earthly
and not too despicable space
reveals a curvature of plan
not ultimately human.

To be illogical is not to be denied
when human measurements are tried

yet logic takes the clue away
from simple, pleasurable certainty.

Who owns the secret, in the end,
ascetic, or brigand?

Chromatism in Red

On every house is red
from sun's descending heart
and every branch and leaf seems to smart
as if itself had bled
away with ruby dying
of first October day.
Restless wing is gently flying
into every face of it,
greedy for each trace of it.

Seasonal luxuries descend, and come
close to every stone, nestle home
within the shadow soft, and the ground
makes plenteous the feel of room
and pleasure for the padded hound.
The grouse goes grazing tips of sumac buds
as if it had the need of ruby floods
within its quick brown eye, and for
its earth-seeking breast, the last warm
of the year takes to its shaken nest.

Brown Gulls

Having sat, and smouldered on himself
two years now, ashes clinging to earth
because ashes are a part of earth
knowing it best because so like
smoke rising out of meagre flame
not rising to heaven, sad because it could
not be so, for smoke that reaches heaven
concurs with given glory in a given time—
alas, smoke not eloquent as that, for smoke
can be beautiful when climbing gloriously
toward glory—but this smoke had not done so,
been so, nothing to make it so,
done nothing but clogged eyes, stifled breath,
smudged air with defeats, inflation, remorse;
Brown gulls, feeding on little knick-knacks
of the sea,
washed up to ease some trifling perfidy
of surge and throe, to have it thus, have it so,
when tide is out in search of more tide,
looking like smoke, brown gulls in fumy silhouette,
going nowhere, reminding him of himself,
setting him to wonder too, in passing, where
do gulls go when they want to die,
for no one sees a gull dead, or dying.
He would have been pleased even to have had
his smoke take on the look of salphiglossis
flowers which hold and unfold in folds of smoke-hue
rayed with sea-light morning light.
Everywhere, upon the last alnages of October
thin thrusts of thought came over him,
like his own smoke covering, smarting his eyes
smarting the doorways of his mind
for the work of his mind was made
of seeing mostly, believing that what there is
to see is so much more than what there is
to hear,
as his smoke his eyelids would,
and did.

Wingaersheek Beach

Shell,
sitting still,
whitely, ghastly, immovable
unless wind whip it other way
on white sand whiter in a sandway
than itself
holding, folding, moulding
last curve, ancestral swirl
bleached whiter
lying lighter
for the whiter way, jeopardy
of lying, by wind, sun, mist, rain, bent and torn
sandpeep's breast in flawless emulation
lip in death like it
when death strike it
white
or speechlessness of one
gone white with ashy blight
fear to lose a tithe of it
thing held, from fright of it.

Water from the Rock

O—lead me there
to where pure water gushes forth
from rock made bountiful
with faith.

Let me lie down
to the brown earth
touch there my parching tongue
sweet roots among
lave lips, slake drouth
soothe aching mouth.

From whatever source it come
let that be welcome—
make it sheltering home
to my unquestionable need—
come swifting ere by spirit bleed
itself in aimless death
breathlessness with breath
immingle
wholly to be single.

O—keep my feet from burning
down their trackless track
no gentlest succour spurning
lest the day go black—
I would that I might lift the scar
from all but sightless eye
some piercing shaft of light deploy
to where these lightless barriers are—
I would not walk where wide crevasse
splits earth itself asunder
mass upon splintering mass
myself drawn under.

Cool be thy mercy's flow
river beneath the glowing rock
obstructing not the silver show,
I would not be slow
to sense wonder.

I have not wing to soar
I have not sky to leap
wildly, joyously, like antelope
of heaven with crystalled harnesses
caparisoned,
I have this earthly tryst to keep
as prisoner, garrisoned
among his writhing-stones
bruising his honest bones.

Come, river from the rock
let me the caller and the crier
have the living shock
touch of the undying fire.

New Rains

New rains wash down
young ships that do not
go to sea
and old ships rot
with sodden density
of being rudderless.
I see them out across the night
and note their purposeless
plight.
It is the young ship's hope
that winds will calm
and rains and mists will cease.
What shall the rudderless
be thinking
cool or warm
when keels are sinking?

Rites of Passage

Surprise Package

My youth came to me
long after it was due—
I was an old man
at twenty-two,
childhood being terribly true.

Youth comes at the changing
of the tide
with the swelling of the sea
when things and objects
manifold their beauty.

It all seemed so wonderful.
I never shall be old again,
I said—
or a voice said—within me,
You shall never be old again—
I believed it to the full.

I scaled the mountain,
braved the height—and the look
of things above it,
now it is all as a well-
thumbed book

as the unhinged copy of Ossian
I hold in my left hand,
all this I understand
and understood—
it made me feel good
to learn I love it.

Yielding the Initiative

Yielding the initiative to the
word—
when it comes to the music that
is one thing—
that too can become a small thing
and now we might just as well say—
P.Q.D. means exactly the same
as P.D.Q.

We undress the words, frisk them
give them a bath in a respectable
solution
they come out completely clean—
pasteurised
then they must go back to the old
job
of being sweet and pretty and
gracious and dangerous
useful for murder and lying
therefore useful in business, in
society, even in poetry.
The music is sure, but the word
has gone hunting for another
meaning across some fashionable
meadow
another meaning that will look
like honesty—sincerity—
the initiative has been yielded
without mercy.

John Donne in His Shroud

It was a smart caprice
to dress
you like this.
Was it a borrowed occasion
as some hire evening suits
for a party?

And the white poppy
on top of your head,
does that mean now white
that it once was red?
For red is the color of a pagan wine
of brisk desire
and of flesh-fire—
white is for calm attire.

In any case, if it is character
is wanted in a face
I would say—look at
John Donne,
that will suffice,
fierce passion turned to ice
and frozen light.

■

Somewhere, between the coming
and the going
there seem to be two wings, always
cutting wind
they spring, to break away
the drift from the blowing
leaving it somewhat glowing—
with sense of decency between
the knowing—and the not knowing
the amity through simple bargains
makes plain
the thin sharp line—
that is quintessentially—
kind.

American Ikon—Lincoln

I have walked up and down the
valleys
of his astounding face
I have witnessed all the golgothas
I have climbed the steep declivities
of all his dreams
listened to the whickering of the
wind
around them
like a lilliput I have sat, quietly
upon his haggard chin
looked up at the breaking rain
falling from his furrowed lids.
I have for once heard God calling
all things to order here.
I have seen infinite mercies
on his woman's lower lip
in the same way I have seen
determination
upon his man's upper.
Pity has poured out from between
these massive portals
majesty of love has walked out
of them
clothed in amazingly decent garments
the only voice worth hearing has sounded
great beauty in my ear
because I have walked where I have
walked
I have scaled the sheer surface of his
dignities
watching the flaming horizon
with calm.

197

V—Is for Victory as You Can Plainly See

I never really like this cat though she is
a valuable asset to this household.
Everybody smiles and is pleased when she
rolls over on a mouse—and if she gets a
rat by the back of the neck she drags him
in until somebody has noticed her skill
then she will chew off its head.

She does far worse than this—she
catches birds and it makes no difference
how the family frowns—she pays no
attention
to it—
She has just caught a little bird and killed
a song—it flutters a little in her
tightened jaws,
I try to get it loose but suddenly I see the
head lean back—give up the ghost—
In each of the cat's eyes is a vast V.
No more songs now in the waving grass.

If It Were the Eye

If it were the eye
that solely were to satisfy
then we could easily say
what all but faultless blazonry
but when the mind begins to work
then everything goes dark
as very often is the way
the heart no longer knows to breathe
spitting instead of pumping blood
as it does.

8 Words

To
spin
a rapture
high
is
solar
sanctity.

A Word and Its Meaning

How wonderful it is to say
one word—knowing one means it
perfectly.
With the best of intentions there is—
the word.
We yield to its instinct initiative
it starts to go into its place
the look is like the shape and
the shape like the look
one gets the feeling—here is
the miracle—about to happen.
The word and its meaning
have fallen in love—
the marriage in heaven is about
to happen.
Suddenly—
there is a sad look in the face
of the word—
it has lost its courage
and we come again to that terrible
old cause of confusion—
conversation.
Sometimes it seems as if we
really couldn't bear the
miracle
saying one single word—
meaning it—perfectly.

Dusty Cousin

There Are No Names

*"There are no names for those things
amongst which one is completely alone."*
Valéry

WE do not go—we stay—
the body takes a certain ride
from the gullible outside
to the intelligent inside.
Earth takes back charitably
what it so casually gave
and the place is called with
simple persiflage—the grave.
Leaves drop off—fruits come
down
the compost cherishes an excellent
renown—
but WE? we stay as certainly
as what gives up goes willingly
after sense and its tender recompense
have done with composite quibbling
and the worth is severed from
the THING
and youth that was thought so
lamentably to pass
merely revives its comprehensible
franchise.
Therefore youth is something that
we never lose
after bone and flesh have served
a use
heaven but the aspect of the
intercession—
calling for no contrition.

■

Vast rose of July
exuding the best there is of sumptuous
summer
the bay leaves soaking in the sea-meanings
rich odour springing from them
when rubbed between the hands
orients promiscuous evolving—
begin again they say—begin again—
drop human machination
brain wants something more than
concepts of men
mankind now in dastardly huddle
and the heart taut double
with desperate trouble.

Logic

Understanding the logic of
simplicity presupposes a
considerable relationship to it
which makes us unafraid to
encounter and endure it.
It nourishes us with its own
sumptuous banquet.

Moralizing

The signature of our behavior
defines the depth of its impression.

Plover

I held him in my unspeaking hand
after the shot struck him
and saw his eyes close down upon
an emaciated world
I could feel his breath leaving his
body
his breast sinking slowly as the last
sigh left him
blood of the lamb at Eucharist was
on his shop-worn wings.
I could hear the stop of the wind
in his wings
Sunday morning over the waves—
the ding-dong of them made
flayed, mortician music
none of the mourners were paid
or price exacted.

This Millimeter

This millimeter of synthetic experience
which because of defect in articulation
some so glibly call, God—
like the fish-hawk above the cove
inscribing uncompleted circles
fearful lest those imaginary beings
called—the dead
in the little cemetery on the hill
smothered with wild roses
should lift a dusty eyebrow and
remark—poor bird
deluged with uncompleted circles as
we ourselves smothered with wild
roses
we have all tried them once—from the
apex of the north pole to the crusty
edges of the Orizabas of our
untutored imaginations
we have sniffed the gardenia and
the magnolia of our faulty conceits
we have stroked the edges of the pyrites
and the blocks of sulphur and amethyst
in geological museums
like the fish-hawk above the cove
like the triangles of geese and the
long parades of dark ducks to the
south of our withered dreams—
in other words we have inscribed
our insurrections acutely and found
them rusty at the brakes.

■

Whoever dies—dies for the love
of beauty—
no matter what the shape, the sense
is there,
for there is obviously beauty—everywhere.

The mole with its 22 tentacles smells
out the loveliness of the worm beneath
the earth—
the weasel sucks its victim's blood
then eats its brains—
what morsel to wrap a thin tongue
around!
Even the rat knows sweet tenderness
of love—
the raccoon teaches its young to
wash the food it eats.
Everything dies for love of
something better
a loose—or a lost ideal—
precision of the letter.

Little Green Snake

The little green snake would thank
me if it could
because I so thoroughly understood
for it is always "over there" or
just beyond
of which everything and every of us
are fond—
I said, green thing, if you will go
straight the way I show
you will again find grass
and shadows luminous.

I could hear the thunders of the
black wheels down the road.
You expect me to go the "straight"
way, it said
looking up, discomfited.
I, a thing that lives by spiral
turns, melodious dictation,
"go straight"—
it would so terribly mean that I
would be dead
that way, for all things go that way
to their last bed—
but something said to it, be nice
go straight as ever you can
for that is very human.
Ten minutes' labour on the liver's
part
sent joy into his very heart,
he found sweet grass 'neath gentle
honied vines
where its silken behaviour now
shines—
to cross the black, black road
that was his heavy, heavy load.

Courage for Lost Poems

Lost poems live a better
life maybe —
than when or if they come to
print.
Leaves fall, and no one wonders
what they do at all
but they alone are wise
with their explicit premises
and if a given rhythm ends
a something wonderfully else begins.
If poems lost could bear the
same profound import
as leaves when wind is done
with them
they would but do a better job
possibly
than if they were cloaked with glory.

Miscellaneous Late Poems

Yes, I Know—Yes

That luscious look of something becoming
something else in front of one which is
the grandest aspect of all—ourselves
intercepted by something not—
therefore—the revelation.
The raison d'être of equanimity brushed
by the dawn-wing of natural piety
therefore that luscious look of something
like Friday becoming something like Saturday
even before the midnight sets in—
well it is the arbiter of our just
retirement—
or, well—isn't it?
O yes, I know—yes.

At Half Past Anything

At half past anything—O how green
everything is—full of the best acres of
delicate promise.
The July blooms swinging in among shifts
of dew and sudden morning
the cows grazing on new heathers and the
sea throwing over extatic swells,
the fiddle-head forms now swaying like so
many exact arrow points and the new
little shells from Pine Point full of the
very flesh of the sea,
and when you eat these infant clams
you know you have the sea in you
as when you have eaten the campestris
you know the fine flavor of earth in you,
we wishing to be as glib as the terns
and the petrels—free, free, free, of
everything
the wave our coach and something floating
over a seven-course meal.
O at half past anything exactly
would be really most wonderful.

Cicada

Cicada rubs its wings and makes a
plangent sound
like tympanies, too soon struck, and previously
awakened
from some imaginary, marvelled sleep,
as if some heaven-tryst to bravely keep—
thrush holds golden note until the very
end
then sends it forth to meet the going sun
when worth of highspent day is done.
Night brings in the droning of the whip-or-will
beneath the branches of the bearded willow tree
then suddenly—even night itself is still.
I hear the murmur of all those salutary things
when statutory word is spoken
then will I know that all the world is woken
to live another life from dawn to
dark
and dark to dawn
when majesty of dream is won.

Reflex

The macabre simplicity of the white church
across the road in which never a prayer is
formed nor antiphon sung
seagulls and starlings perching on the roof-tree
in hastily devised rows, the tall and the short of
it in modified black and white
swallows with sunflush on their hearts swooping
up and down the temporal pattern, like drunken
punctuation—
July's sentence stiffly spoken against August's
too decisive recitation
with its wands of fire-weed if the clarion
call has come too soon
are months at times in a hurry to get it
over with too—we have known them too
who have dreamed too drunkenly.
O whip of any little wind,
drive toward our bleak simplicities the
tender thoughts we beckon to us
that we may unarm them in unfaltering love.

And Now—September

And now September, where is summer gone.
It always seems as if summer must stay
a long, long time—it never does, it goes away.

Where does summer go—what's it like
where it has gone—does it fall among
dismantled springs, gathering to itself
resurrection clothes,
does it have the same niceness—the look
of bright everlastingness which when it
is here it has—or we think it has?

When summer is here among us, we act
that way ourselves, adopt summerish
opulence
as if nothing could intervene
with the long day of our sumptuous scene
and the very flesh of us expands to a bronzed
usefulness.
Then comes the knock in the head—
the way split open—the laughter of promises
crushed—
summer—taken away by some irresponsible
mortician—and the several birds saying
we must go too—wherever summer goes.

The Flight

The flight of the bird—any bird—measuring
distance by fragments of time well studied
as to the tax and the tempo
the hummingbird who in October at the north
thinks of hibiscus in Mexico and flies
then from corolla to corolla
we hearing soft tendernesses of time falling
like rain dropped from leaf to leaf
counting the multiple refractions of
radiant disaster
hushing the pressure of our explicit beliefs
almost turned to icicles stiffening on their
every mood with mountains of recalcitrant
decision in their whitened blood
bringing all back with them from the thick
shadows of Orizaba, all but drowned in
the breath of the last word in flowers.

Word Arrangements for Pictures by Morris Graves

1. Little Bird Alone

It is nothing that you think it is
little bird alone —
only the shrived thoughts about your head
and folded wing
make it imperative to do something about
all this and do it devoutly.
But I can tell by the slightly falling curve
at the end of your bone mouth
that you have had converse with illimitable
framed integrities
and they have left a twist in your tongue
once cleft with some decent arpeggios
of song —
Everything goes through this one time or
another
when, to speak plainly — an interval is
broken
we note the two ends — one where it left
off and the other where it must begin again
the space between being that simple,
elegant matter called Loneness —
we have learned how sacred that alone
is.

2. Eagle of the Inner Eye

It would be bound to be like this
with so much wound up to be
let down again like the spring of a
cheap clock.
I see a singular shuttle of time
weaving back and forth between two
attenuated retinas
and I am amazed things are as livable
as they are
for, after all, something must be done
about something all the time
even though the heats of quiet matters
do something to take the frost from the
blade.

How many times have I been shot through
(and loved the very bullet) with these piercing
intimations
and have been quite willing to take it
for I have always known that every one
must be shot through (and love the bullet
too).
It is just this that makes us know
exactly how perfectly well off we are—
to be shot through—
but O—it is the bullet that must be
loved.

3. Little Known Bird of the Inner Eye

I'm telling you now, that if you keep
on like this, you will see yourself
through to a spacious palatial freedom.
We must be ready to pack up like
a common vagabond
to get over on the other side of the stark
torrents that plunge under our tissued
bridges.
Like a traffic cop at theatre-out time
of some desultory March evening
we must push the impertinent interval
to its plastic conjugations—
there must be arm-wavings and hand
up-liftings with large white gloves
in the forty-fourth street Subway manner
they must get across, they must get
across
with feet or wheels not planted in
secular aftermath
as yours might seem to be when
questioned with propriety.
I have studied well the geography of the
inner eye and noted all its precepts.

Buttons for Swallows

I think now and then of the old family button
bag which I could paw over when I wanted
to.
They had the shine of swallows scooping up a
breeze—dark radiance of peacock feathers
something of tinker mackerel when they lie
over to make a school turn in the water.
There was a romantic scene on these buttons
a sort of Claude Lorrain kind of view.
The story of willow ware everybody knows—
castle to the left—tree to right—of a lake—
the two lovers could not leave the palace, so
something said they could be birds, so changed
them into that, and they flew away across
a quiet sky.
I like the swallows that sit on telephone wires
or steering in and out of old barns.
Then comes the day when they suddenly fly off
the wires and out of lofts and go down south
to be gay.
I remember how the scene on the buttons was
exactly like an iridescent Claude Lorrain
but I would always give buttons for swallows.

Ichneumon

Ichneumon laid its egg
upon the pulse of dream
the edges withered, leaving
but the shattered theme,
Ichneumon
nothing could live because
Ichneumon had settled in.

How many a warm dream
is stilled
and many a smile is chilled
and killed
before the throne
Ichneumon.

Segment after segment touched
joy after joy crutched
limping away to shadow spot
where misery is not.

This Piece of Eucharist

This piece of Eucharist falling gently
upon the lips of the young soldier on
his knees in green grass "somewhere on
Irish soil"—
who can tell to what place the divine flavor
will come?

When I saw the late September moonlight
rising over the anlage of the early evening,
it came to me, this is the whole of the
piece that fell upon the young soldier's lips.
He would feel better—his soul would find
a moment's peace
but would he know more—could he tell more
than he knew before—no nothing—and for
this piece of Eucharist he was devoutly
thankful.

What we know is tiresome because what
is on the surface is merely the scale of
the fish, and does the scale know the
wild perception of the fish itself?
No nothing—but it is nevertheless happy.

Immortal Face

It was a long time ago—but everyone says
it was true.
A pretty young girl engaged to a handsome young
man and they loved each other dearly;
one day pretty girl was taken sick and she
knew she wouldn't live very long and so it
was she died one day.
Before she died she called her beautiful
lover to her and said—after I am gone you
must go to the graveyard and there in the
marble stone you will see my face and
after a while he was astounded because, sure
enough, the face of his beloved appeared
upon the marble stone.
He went back to the people and told his story;
many believed him and many said he had
lost his mind.
So they decided to go and see for themselves
and the sight was in a way terrifying but
beautiful as ever, for there they saw
the pretty face of the young girl outlined
upon the marble stone
and then they knew the handsome young man
was sane and in his right mind
and to this day people go there and come away
rewarded.

Beauty is something that you see where you
want to see it and where you want it
to be.
We who live by what we see
in the mirror of our hasty days compel
a strange propensity.

218

K. von F. — 1914 — Arras-Bouquoi

"by the haste of a cruel stop, ill-placed"
Robert Crashaw

Man in perfect bloom
of sixfoot splendour
lusty manhood time — all made of youthful fire
and simplest desire,
voiceless now these many years —
what music in the voice that was,
beyond all calumny of tears.

What makes it seem
as if you never went away
what gentle gleam from out
the perfidy of wars
gives hint of immortality?

In dream I saw you once
all made of living fire —
clothed in lightning's wondrousness
there to cherish, there to bless —
the light flew up my willing side
and filled me with fraternal pride,
all made of pristine fire
you were,
symbol of your natural attire;
Yourself the moment that I saw
and took into my heart
is still an image that I worship —
not death but love inspire
to keep this everlasting fellowship.

Find the Face

Shall we ever find the face again,
the face of things that once we thought
was beautiful?
Shall we ever learn to piece together
the cracked bits put up on the frozen
wall of our innocent beliefs,
looking for the missed curve that made
the features whole—
shall we ever find the face again?

Shall we ever find the hand again
that held our own so warm and made
it glad
the flipped finger turning over the pages
of our fixed thoughts
turning over the split stone of our
ancient contentions
smeared now with the scent of dirty
dreams
the froth of maniacal mouths spewed
upon our shut lashes
blinding the world from faced complexities
tearing nothing but gutturals from the throat?

■

It was to learn that grief is a major
matter,
so shocking, so throttling to the senses
or
any other picture of life—
striking as it did at the center as a bolt
of lightning does on a rock,
splintering this way and that—subsiding
in its own terrific flare, clearing its own
smoke
leaving the fissure in the rock wide and
dark in its width—this too the human
heart
all too honest and therefore crucifying
striking the decent place in us
sheltering the auroras of our childish
instincts and intuitions.
Struck down, the woman and the man
in a heap of this—we thank the Lord
for this that Thou hast given us—
stroking the felled branches of their tree
together.

Blessed Event

She is again with child
she with the clear face—mild
like morning with an evening veil
air is rife with festival.

He hurried to her bulging side
from a long far diffident place.
He too lovely with young man's
loveliness.

Here two clear roses
on spring begotten stalk
there are two buds beneath
their tenderest shade
act of love's exquisite shock.

Several Pieces for Jose Garcia Villa

1.

Like a lustrous bird threading the maze
of sunlit morning flowers
he swirls from the moment's to the hour's
dear-bought simplicity
he dreams—dwells as sudden day's scant
gravity
making sign of something like cross upon
the brow of every fancy that is freed of
labors for its own reward.

I shall live most certainly, he said,
my own quick life—separately,
I have not time to live the shape
of other lives,
I must keep sacred honour that it gives
to live with silence stark and proud
serenity.
The dream—it is a caustic harsh
severity
and lets the brush of its translucent wings
disturb the lip of every minstrel in distress
questioning the worth of ultra-cogent things.

Be brave, young ardent flaming man
and take it nobly if you can
splendour is a sharp-flamboyant danger
for either friend—or stranger.

2.

Villa—I would be brief, yet say—
you know the fierce poetic arms of Love
how it bled away the full ventricle of a
decent heart—
the smouldering visions of rich Salinas
and many another with strict sure sense
of salutary recompense
birds nesting on a crown of thorns, or
upon the cleft edge of the universal wound
the laceration of the holy rose pressed

harshly into silent hair
the fingers tipped with potent dreams
touched with cooled encomiums
the glint from a frog's eye peering out of
thickened floating green
upon fresh verdure of the sweetened scene.
Villa—you have it
keep it—with specific acumen.

Albert Ryder—Moonlightist

Moonlight severing his ancient mariner's
beard
and falling over the cliffs of his eyebrows
his lips fearing to touch what was no
longer available
night streaming through his listless fingers
with the texture of impassible days to come
hanging like limpid moss from his prophet
shoulders—
this beautiful man, suffering from the weight
of majesty of dream
because he had been denied substance of
any other truth—dream so sumptuous—heavy
with failures of death radiant with shimmer
of new belief.
I am speaking of Albert Ryder moonlightist
as I knew him—
"I asked him to Christmas dinner," the lady
said to me, who had a long time known him,
"he said he would come, we waited two hours
for him—the party eager to see him—he did
not come."
Next time she saw him—"O we were so
disappointed you did not come"—
"I was there," said Ryder, "I looked through the
window—saw the lovely lights—it was very beautiful."

Eilshemius

If you had sat with Eilshemius
quieted him with silence or calmed
words
you have seen thin rays of moonlight
quiver on his lips—noted the vast
miseries he suffered—crucifixion of
loneliness—heard the newspapers rattle
upon his chest—try them—they will keep
you warm he said to a famous woman
painter—
"When she died"—meaning his loved one—
"I thought I couldn't live she was so
beautiful
suddenly out of the window I saw the moon—
and I said to myself—I can live for that—
that is beauty"—
It was the sun that forgave and forgot
him.

Marianne Moore

Like a surgeon at the drugged decisive
table
opening the cicatrice carefully, to find
what ails the sentence—separate fruit
from rind
the sickness of the hyper-trammelled theme
or shake the skeleton of a proved factitious
thought
noon-high with genteel cool perspicacity
heart left to fend for itself since it
is not asked to even speak its piece
for casual concordance of timed release
benight her—we might add—for keeping poetry
from bending fallacious knee or breathe
too heavily in areas conspicuously forlorn
for which it was never born.

Concert

If, in search of a given honesty
you seek in certain passages of
Mozart—the relation of the pianist to the
notes, and you find his fingers most of all
interested in his fingers,
the phrases turning sort of mountebank
as he covers them with glib hands, and
irrelevant smiling, saying to himself
was it not beautiful, how I waited for the
orchestra to give me those passages for
myself which I have claimed for myself,
perhaps, which, if the composer, he—MOZART
were living, he might in all honesty say,
I should really like some of this for
myself, would the pianist be kind enough
to give a certain moment to Mozart
for himself—just for himself?

Heifetz—On the Air, Bell Telephone Program

Wolves howling against the lips of
midnight birds
thrashings of wild fowl upon a bitter wind
spitting on young volcanoes coughing in a
rush of sun
cast-iron pianissimos simulating the
mulched recitation of some cynic flying
throat
death-dealing wonders of majestic tone.
It seemed as if I had heard some ice-bound
bell crack in some crevassed city of the
moon
as if my veins had emptied hard-earned blood
in diminished places
or as if a thrush had poised itself on my
right shoulder singing—nothing doing,
nothing doing—I cannot tell you where
you go from here—
different wines spill from different bottles—
I felt a turgid breeze break as if from
magyar throats pushed out—across my
rigid brow
leaving me plenty of the here—and now.

Vanquished in a very plain degree
far beyond the sense of frenzied extasy
pressed into a sphere of smouldering elegance
hoping to connive with circumstance.

Listening to the Music

Listening to the music of the waters
the dash of little waves that will,
not long to wait, be greater
children of the deluge, unlearned of
their terrific power
playing about like lion cubs over
the loins of these stone lionesses
blinking against the light of the mid-
day hours
the bobbing up and down of white breasts
that seem as if they would lash the air
itself with clothy tongues
trickling back at the feet of the impregnable
sphinxes
that have no mysteries to disclose because
for all silent things there is no mystery
they in their silence having dissolved it
and—
Listening to the music of the waters
we learn we can face something and
nothing a great deal more than we
thought we could.

■

We have broken bread
with many a stranger wild
the seagulls said—
we shall break bread
with tomorrow's child
before we to paler cliff
have fled.

Mole

Little morsels of smoothed grey energy
learning the secret of fresh burrowing
called to other order by major dip
of claw—
Blindness is nothing to a mole
it is the terrible gift of seeing that
hurts,
it is not alone legs that ache—it is
press on breast bone
all done for—without even lustre of
desire.
Mole cannot catch earthworm nor means
of light involve
so may face terrible beauty keeping eye
open too long
and you—what possible use could you
be having for it?

To Partridge Merrithew

Dear Partie—
You are of course a bird and that is why
I assume that so many want to fly with
you.
I saw a brown rooster strutting on a rock
the other day—tail all out like a fan
ruffs up—and it came to me—yes
that yourself—flying to some smooth
covert—
never suspecting that to be truly alone one
must drive headlong into a milling crowd.
Have I not seen the loveliest life in the
great crowds of the many high-spots
in the world—
and if it was minuit de Noel—suddenly
a rushing somewhere, and everyone was
gone awhile and each countenance then
different—having made peace with the
all promising moment—beginning again
to do the same thing—over again.
O—Partie—nothing like clandestine marriage
with a crowd
you learn to feel so completely out loud
in a crowd.

The Very Languor

The very languor of the morning
showing August is preparing
for death because now sleeping.
The crowing of the bantam—
the red cheek of a single dahlia
the fluttering of the wash on the line
against the vastness of the
horizontal of the sea—
how terrifying at times a flat
line can be—
or the crowing of a bantam
with red cheek of a dahlia.
The very languor of the morning
is also—so.

Serving the Curve

Serving the curve of this coast
the wind lazes along, winding
itself among the perched starlings
on the weather vane of the defunct
church
ospreys swing low and high at
the west uttering guttural enchain-
ments of sounds
the gulls gaffing fish talk too.

Inner Distance

Strange place—where all men gain
their courage to be their inebriate selves
singular point of departure where all things
come up to the very retina and depart again
among the stupidities and the objective joke.
Inner distance—that is the place extraordinary
where speech begins—thoughts without words
pure peace—when the heart and the mind
are removed from words.

I remember once I could not speak words
I never remember such happiness.
I felt as if I [were] bargaining with defunct
meteorites that kept the dignity they found
when they fell.
When I put my hand on the willemite as
innocents touch fingers to a font in a
plunked ritual—
I know I have touched supremacy—because
it fell and never spoke of its falling.

Encompassed

Encompassed me in arms
concentric—
took kin and left me happy
free
eyes burned like flames in burning
tree
tongue clogged with exquisite fury.

Hair stood on end like fury-fire
mouth blowing steam of thick desire
we will go, you will go, you will
not go, without me.

I will be thunder in your stride
I will be terror in your thickening
eyes—wide
with stricken wonder.

I will be love
you never heard of
and shoots of everlasting fear-
lessness
will break from your engendered
breast
ere sun go to west
you will be utterly encompassed.

I walked along
beaten with the song.

Three Loving Men

Adelard, Etienne
consummate men
each loving each,
each loving me, and then
showing these in a dream
of men.

We will build a house
they said—make it safe
from rain
said Adelard, Etienne.

Black went the sky
pale went the house
wind tore it out of rafter
death dancing after
house fell to ruin
for three men.

I alone am loving
two consummate men
who will not come again
because two are not now
breathing men
Adelard, Etienne.

O Bitter Madrigal

The ventricles of his heart burst
like a dyke upon the world of his
simple things
and the blood of his being flooded the
fields and valleys, leaving wide wake
of grief upon parched places of earth
O bitter Madrigal!

Sing not O bird upon my shoulder. I have
no ear for sensed logic of peace. I am
broken in two—the world and the dream
split in two—the rags of them trailing over
my aching bones, my lips suppurate with
gall
O merciless madrigal!

Who is there will come to tell me how
to live—letting flag of joy furl out
as once it did, over my trailing hair,
over my feet, soothing the tips of my
fingers with gentleness:
I float, faint, fall
O bitter madrigal!

My son! my son! bred from my once
quiet flesh and wholesome bone
his dream dismantled, his new breath
trampled on,
his smile like twisted trusting leaf
by hands made of steel and ice, washed
with lyric tears
heart and limbs that once were bright
and warm
now parcelling to dust—O dream! O faith!
O love! O beauty broken!
cease pouring into my ears—bird on my shoulder
this anguish, this blood-strewn agony
nothing now be done to make me free
my son forever gone—from me!

O merciless madrigal!
O bitter madrigal!

■

Fantasy and phantom—
everything in passionate search
of something to remember—then
for a long time—forget.
We can take the poets with a grain of salt
nothing is as different as the poets
make it,
nothing as regionally impeccable as
the poets make it—
and yet—
the something they could not say
despite their glibly flowing words
falls and furls from the firs and
the hemlocks, the spruces and the
granite declivities
like ripples from a seablown flag
revealing the stout complexion
of geographies—the places with names
like windstruck persons
the very bone of location rattling
against the sea-thrown breeze—
and there—the residue of meanings—
crystals dug from the dark of the
earth
substances revealed,
and there—the miracle of
place.

So it is—
when I look at the Androscoggin
sauntering quietly along like
statesman to his problems
and watch the wind blow up little
waves upon the tumultuous Kennebec
into minuscule throe of froth
it comes—
it doesn't matter what men do
above the surfaces—
they themselves remain inscrutable
ignoring sentiment—factitious extasy

they live the lives of dark
contemptuous waters—
and the things men do—do nothing
to—them.

"Vacationland"—
the word shivers down the spine
like lightning in among the spruces
and the firs
shaking the earth from the root—
and the river waters and the sea
waters laugh like cynic loons
who shriek derision as they dive
beneath the surfaces of removed
waters beneath the staggered mountain.

What would Thoreau see
if he took another look at his
sacred Walden today?
laughter of the loon,
travesty of ulterior devotion
nature—abhorring
the vacuum.

There are, in reality
"no names for things among which
one is quite alone."

There Are No Rocks and Trees

There are no rocks and trees that take
the place of people
the people that are rich and round and large
strong with a nation's agitation
deep with a lovingness profound—
I wouldn't know what a tree can do
how much of love it brings
of what peculiar extasy it sings
but when my eye can sweep the glory-ridden space
where people walk or stand, there are no rocks and trees
to take their ultra-loving place.

Perusing Mallarmé in Maine

Mallarmé,
with this equestrian cliff clutching
at sky-reins hyper-fervently
protecting ponderously the fragrant
width of words,
wind pounding sea-froth into frozen
curds
against the curves of sleek, world-without-
end wandering birds,
words fragile, if you will, but as most
fragile things, profound,
yet following in grooves the still
insensate ground,
thought leaping after fleet anxieties
of subtle sense,
pursuing soft compensatory ways
though they but seem as driftwood,
heart-stunned hordes.

"Yielding the initiative to the words."
Sound recompense with breath of poetry
for clue,
desperate the sheen of truth craving
to be true
climbs precipice of pride but then,
like shattered plunder among men,
to fall and downwardly disperse
and take a seawashed, throat-filled vow
between a then, and now.

How true a poet is,
contrives a sheaf of centuries
a branch will break, a stone will roll
away,
and then the poet builds his day.

Recognition of Region

I kissed the rock near which
I lay—beneath a range of seasoned blue
Mother I said—
I have been desultory but true
worn key
of flagrant extasy
upon a clanking chain
only because I knew
though my breast bone burned too
often
something would the burden soften.

All round the iron road of everywhere
I overwisely wandered
I thought it would
to me show whole of paradise
until I thought twice—
but good enough for me I learned
the place so early spurned.
How could it else but home be
that took so long to see.

My mother has a handsome face
all veined with granite strength and grace
where every wind-seared cicatrice
shows battle and a world of love
powerful but gentle as perhaps the dove
as often is—at home.
How proud I was of mother-welcome.

Back Road Country

In this house there are swallows
resting upstairs.
In the farthest rafters
they have with rich cups of clay
mouthful by mouthful made them
strong for their destiny.
You see the print of their swallow
lips laid row on row.
There are rakes and plows and sleds
sitting silently, cluttering old sheds
where back bone meets breast bone
of each conglomerate skeleton.
The plow will never meet the furrow
the sled will never see the snow,
where futility now beams through.

Festoons of tethered moth and grey
illiterate fly
bespeak in accents moribund
the crude festivity.
The weather here will never find
its east or west
or north or south
for everything is sunken to its knee
in homely travesty.
Wild mint comes wafting over
brake and flag
where senile lintels sag,
a pony cart in devastated blue
a phaeton in calico dismay
await some touch of useless charity.
Yet somehow furtively
these effigies in clutches of decay
bespeak coolly touch of recognition
to soften their perdition.
The paper on the wall is ignominious
brown,
yet when the sun goes affluently down,
over river, mead, and then the mountain,
these walls light up pathetically

as of a long stilled voice just spoke
and everywhere are touches to evoke
a day, an evening and a night
when common things were far less
erudite.
I hear the "hermit" from out the darkened
wood
give accent to the evening wood
as if he thought there must be touch
of song
for everything gone wrong.

Beyond the Broken House

Two horses
white,
in the gathering moonlight
stood
and a dark one grazed
between.
They fed upon a purpling sward
and on the transitory lunar flood
at ending of a field that seemed
an almost green
where little flashlights here and there
had gleamed.

A spinsterish wraith of mist was seen
to gather up itself above close by vagrant
wood
where sunlight once had been.
Two hours ago this was, the sun had shone
before the day was done
and scene was filled with endless
mood.

Two horses
white
in the shifting moonlight
seemed to stare
where bleaching boards with ashy
grey
were covered and nothing that could there be said
would soften strange duplicity
as yawning windows mouthed their
stark consent—
the darker horse revealed a dark
assent,
and as the rows of flattened grass
there hovered
their gleams of glass-like emerald
remorse
as if to make a recovery of whitened

white
and gave no clue to where the daylight
went.
The night declaimed its mightiest
resource,
and certain banishment.

The Pilgrimage, and the Game Warden

He brought me to the foot of the
scarp,
the postillions of reverence riding ahead
of him—
he that had Ktaadn in his flesh
and bone,
and the look of windbeaten eyries in his
eyes—
wings that have battered many a thunder-
ridden cliff—
sweeping his priest-like nostrils
and the pale wash of many a proud
interval of rain, upon his hyper-
weathered cheek—
he that had seen the place of the evening sun
upon the troubled stone
long before his infant hands had
reached for the palings of his cradle.
I know the world because I have
kissed the roots of flowers,
and have stroked many an evening bird
to its gentle sleep.
I have heard the lisping of imperious waters
and the last rumblings of impetuous
thunders have fallen from my shoulders
in many an inclement hour.

We passed through the vast momentums
of heaped up days fallen in a huddle
at the untoward rush of night—
the plight of massive semitones of
innocent belief fairly crying at us
crossing from alp to alp beneath on
stricken feet.
I couldn't guess the beauty of a night like
this,
until new skies broke again and the sun
threw up its trumpets from a mordant
patriarchal east.
Ktaadn stood like wilful orizabas

unaccustomed to such praise of fretful
minutiae.
The moment of a man clawing at a cliff
is nothing to a cliff.
It is the man that bursts with enmity
toward something bigger than himself—
the whisper of a mountain floors him
suspending his ankles to a laughing
wind.

What Have We All—a Soliloquy of Essences

What have we all, we
who have nothing left but longing to be free
of our lashed satiety.
The world has shapes we never
saw before.
The angles once familiar
broken
split into alien integers
forsaken
bit by bit, the once endearing touch
we saw
like bright veins upon wet leaf
showing now curves of our grief
now chaff blown from the sheaf,
suffering the explicit torture of being awake
for imagination's sake
in order not to feel
press of grinding wheel—
what love
costs more to prove
than heart being torn
from the vision?

These beautiful wild untamable
creatures
dying to keep their features
to keep hearts from shivering to death
and bone from its sickened breath
and white decision.

Vesper Hymn for Tuesday and June, after the Visit of Henry Wells

Let us go out into the daylight
of our firm beliefs
regard this decency of rain as
something to be fond of, take to
our hearts,
covet the quick laughter of tumbling
children
covet the rich brown bravery of
northward bird
stand before the majesty of thick flowers
whose every act is corrective to our
dark implications.

Let us go out into the daylight
of our firm beliefs
reject not any decency of sun
the ripple on the gently flowing river—
the curve of new white rose upon the
terraced park shall sanction all our
well-kept innocences
giving us majesty of dream in curve and tone,
making our separated self into one.
The thin span bridge singing songs
with harp-like sweet gentility.

Let us go out into the daylight
of our firm belief
take over lispings of young waterfalls
trillium's conjecture shall our conduct
be
the swelling of the frog-throats pushing
at the mouth of breeze-blown lily
keep watch of river's dusty trend,
shadow keeping secrets of a million themes
brushed by relevant potencies of wind,
leaving it to the heart to keep true time
from all our impecunious theorem—
Master—make way to let relive

our broken tendencies and our stifled
certainties
bring up above our heads with soft-gloved
hands
our sanctioned abnegations
and so, return to energies serene and
simple
taking tests of every smooth extravagance
of dreams
and the found degree of precious interval.

To the Nameless One

You, who have power over
everything obscure
Listen—come over here, sit by
my side
and let me say the things I want
to say—
I want nothing in the way of artificial
heavens—
The earth is all I know of wonder.
I lived and was nurtured in the
magic of dreams
bright flames of spirit laughter
around all my seething frame.

Rembrandt—Rouault—Piero

Who has sounded or again shalt sound
the unmocked glory of their tone—
who shall lay wealth of bloom on
the cheek at the round
as these three myrrh-hung magi have
done.
Finger the face of their pulsing pictures
and feel the warm blood under the skin,
great hearts having universal seizures
breaking open the longing, aching stone.
Monsieur X—the Resurrection, the whole
of self in Rembrandt come to strike the
gong
of infidel belief to shaking itself, lambent
timbres loud and strong—
Events in simulated glass, the pounding
on a bell of bronze.

250

Androscoggin (1940)

Return of the Native

Rock, juniper, and wind,
and a sea gull sitting still—
all these of one mind.
He who finds will
to come home
will surely find old faith
made new again,
and lavish welcome.

Old things breaketh
new, when heart and soul
lose no whit of old refrain;
it is a smiling festival
when rock, juniper, and wind
are of one mind;
a sea gull signs the bond
makes what was broken, whole.

Androscoggin

The Androscoggin
changes nothing of its flowing—
it glides over the deepset ledges,
swirling away beyond Lisbon—
makes the beautiful curve at Topsham,
mingling with the salt sweat of
outer-ocean washes at Merrymeeting Bay.
Nothing is changed,
nothing is different but ourselves
who note the change that brings us back
to nothing changed.

But here *is* a change—
here are the birds sitting zealously alone
beneath the falls at West Pitch, Lewiston—
strange lust for change again;
the birds—the sea birds—
someone says they wait for fish
to fall with the turmoil of the waters,
fish that have played in black waters
among the mountains.

And when I remarked this change someone said:
"you know these birds are now a
menace socially;
they have discovered the blueberry
pastures—they eat the blueberries
from the bushes before the pickers
can get to them."
Sea birds vegetarians—fancy if you can—
looking for the blue beads with wafts
of skybreath clinging to them—
fresh drafts blown down
from the face of the White Mountains.

Who knows—maybe one day, soaring high,
they will see the mountain cranberries
even hawks and eagles do not see—
so much more succulent and seductive
than the bog cranberries—

the little dark red beads the size of
young new peas, growing quietly among
the crisp, curled mosses—
richer because they are closer to the
inference of height, and the substance
of the night and morning.

The sea birds—changing notions and
customs like the rest of us
turning on the taste of herring and cod and bream,
weary of dropping clams and urchins
from a height to crack the shells open,
leaving free the flesh.
This is why the rocks are covered
with shattered shells.

"Lewiston Is a Pleasant Place"

I admire my native city because
it is part of the secret sacred rite
of love of place.
My childhood which was hard, it is always
hard to be alone at the wrong time,
brought seizures of intensity to the years;
the harsh grinding of the mills rang in
my ears for years—and a sordid sort of music
came out of it.
I return to instances that are the basic images
of my life as it now is.

I go back to the Franklin pasture which for
us children was the Asia and Africa of
our first impressions.

Spring—
and myself walking with my father along the
edges of a cool clear stream, gathering water cresses,
trilliums, dogtooth violets, and in
the fall—at times—mushrooms;
white violets and blue, growing on little hillocks
with trailing evergreens and boxberry leaves,
and here and there, pushing up out of the snow,
the arbutus or, as we called them, Mayflowers.

Drama number one,
the image of all that was to come after:
the death of the white kitten—
wrapping it carefully in something soft—
laying it gently in a wooden saltbox—
fastening the lid down—
burying it deep in a hollow, with tears,
and my sister, Lillie May, joining in the rites.

There were toboggans in winter, made of end to end
joined barrel staves, seat in the middle, gliding
dangerously into the Asiatic valleys below.
Scene-shifting a little later, the pasture a
deep, religious memory;

the Androscoggin
forever flowing solemnly through my brain,
coursing in and out of my flesh and bone,
as it still does, sacredly.

There was Dr. Alonzo Garcelon, always known to us
as Dr. "Gasselon," flying through Haymarket Square
behind his racing steed, spitting tobacco juice
as he went; and the amazing vision of his beautiful
daughter Edith, at church of a Sunday morning.
Mamie Straw and Lizzie Janes, sharp images of a day
so somehow past—
Miss Janes at the organ, pumped by a boy at the
back, out of sight—with the Ascension of Christ
over us all in not too good stained glass, as we
sang magnificats and epiphanies—and
"Lead kindly light amid . . ." "Lord now lettest [thou] thy
servant depart in peace, according to thy word."

Skinny Jinny was a tall, dark-clothed woman with
her thin arms akimbo under her black shawl,
wan-white, frightened of the solitudes that
enveloped her being, we children running madly for
home when we saw her—because "she has a butcher knife
under her shawl"—as if she hated little children, and
maybe she did—so many do.

The Canadians came to the city—giving it new
life, new fervors, new charms, new vivacities, lighter
touches, pleasant shades of cultivation, bringing no
harm to the city, bringing what it now has—a freshening
of city style, richer sense of plain living.
Recently I walked the streets of my native city
and there was gaiety in the air.
My thoughts returned to a white house in Howe Street,
a home with green blinds, the front ones always shut,
where a poet of distinction lived, wrote fine poetry,
cooked Savarinesque foods, writing poetry that few knew
the worth of—and almost none know the value, now.
Wallace Gould, if he is still fact, is a man of great
male beauty and gigantic proportions; he is almost a complete
legend to us now, none of us know where he is,

or if he even lives at all.
Gould was, in the careful use of the word, a genius;
he had high vision and plain habits; he was
a great cook, a superior pianist, with a frantic
worship of Byron.
He had image after image in photo of his idol,
and an impressive replica in plaster.

Gould devoted himself to Greek outline, Horatian
simplicity, with pagan notions of the
livingness of the moment.
He cared nothing for traditions, customs, mechanical
habits—lived the quiet life of a thinking being,
worshipping also his foster mother, genial in his
behaviors,
out of which evolved
The Children of the Sun.

The mills and factories that were once gigantic
in the vision of a child, monstrous, terrifying,
prison-like, are now mere objects on the horizon,
just as the garages and the filling stations have become.
The Androscoggin flows by them all, giving them
power through the solemn canals, minding none of
them, going onward because it has business with the sea.
Lumber was once a great industry; we all saw the
log-drives and jams above the falls, tumbling down
over the waters at West Pitch, settling into
jackstraw patterns as they may now be seen in places
like Trois-Rivières in Quebec—these logs later turning
into paper, turning into stockings, extraneous lingerie;
I myself having seen the moment when wood becomes syrup,
then silk.

On the breast of David's Mountain
many an adolescent dream was slain,
later to be snatched from early death
when manhood gave them back their breath
again.

West Pitch at the Falls

For years, so long, I had imagined
the slopes thickly strewn with pines—
could it have been the rising spray from the
falls from the tumbling waters of spring
freshets veiling the scene, making it seem
more heavily wooded than it now is?
We of the place have often seen the river
swell, rise to the bridge, almost carry it
away, as it in times past already has done,
between Lewiston
and lovely Auburn.

Contrasting the scene when as a boy the river
froze and we skated on the edges of the river
above the falls, while the men featured horse racing
in the center up stream; here and there on the
sides, men cutting cakes of ice eighteen inches thick.
I can see when I want to the images of the two
sisters who threw themselves into the tossing
foam, ending the dismal struggle; all of this
before my time, the story of it from the elders
frightening young minds, at the height of the light
brown foam, avoiding carefully the descent to the
tall Niagara.
In and out of the spring freshet foam
appear the long streams of visions to the
height of the iron bridge above—
the faces of those not now there, and yet still visible.
Now—
gulls gather on thin strips of earth near the
falls, as if talking of old times.

Family Album in Red Plush

My father was an English Yankee who emigrated
from the Wuthering Heights section in eighteen-sixty.
He had very blue eyes and kept these his windows
washed clean; he watched the coronation parade
of plain virtues every day, and let his blue flag
furl out in fine ripples.
He came to Maine when he was a freshly marriageable
young man—to the English colony of Lewiston,
sent for my mother, Eliza Jane Horbury of Stalybridge
near Manchester, and in due time she came over in a
sailing vessel that took six weeks to make the port of Boston;
soon they were married in Victorian cloth and silk.
Nine children were eventually seen to be flocking about the
gateway, and of these I, the last, left to fumble the
latch, period now to a not too ravishing sentence.
I have polished that period with my sleeve to the best
of my ability—I still inhale the yellow Scotch roses,
the tansy down the path, the sweet alyssum and the bleeding
    heart.
My people were good, therefore they were good; that nobody
could deny; and being good, got a nice piece in the paper
when they went, and a sheaf of wheat with a sickle, with
letters of purple straw on a white satin ribbon.

My father was a dreamer—dreamed everything but the right
thing, leaving it to my mother to put his dream in order
and so she took shovel and pick and dug the ditches free.
My father was a cotton spinner from the Lancashire cotton belt.
Then he was bill-poster for my cousin Horbury who owned
the local theatre for forty years, who was an interesting
but thoroughly disliked man. He was handsome with red beard
and high red hair rising from his stiff forehead.
I can still see him talking in front of the bank at the
head of the street with the three Ricker brothers of Poland
Springs, and we may be sure they settled many local things—
they too with long beards looking like Yankee Brigham Youngs.
So my father posted the long handsome bills for Joe Jefferson
in The Rivals and Rip Van Winkle, Margaret Mather in
Shakespeare—Modjeska, Januscheck, Booth, Barret, McCullough,
somebody Kean in Nick of the Woods, Ullie Ackerstrom in

Fanchon the Cricket—I can remember being thrilled when she
came through a window in rags with a real live hen under
her left arm, which as a little boy I thought was great acting.

My father was an average citizen—he voted Republican right
down to thc sound of "earth to earth"—he loathed cigarettes
as an invention of the devil, and smoked a pipe in the middle
of the night.
My father belonged to the street-cleaning squad to the
Royal House of Heaven,
and kept his brooms and brushes clean, polished highly his
name plate on them;
he did not sing hymns around the house but he acted them,
"my soul doth magnify the Lord, and my spirit—"
and my mother scrubbed many a sacred corridor in the Holy
House of the mind. They were excessively human—they
had an almost unnatural sense of bounden duty.
I have spent my life looking through their windows; I send
them flowers tied with severe ribbons in cosmic shades.

Once upon a time my father thought he could be a breeder
of horses, got as far as three, one of them a pet that tried
to get in at the kitchen door. He wore a horse's tooth in
his ascot when he went to be photographed, also a scrubby
mustache, browned in the middle from pipe smoking.
Once in my infancy he bought three bear cubs from a hunter
and put them to the breasts of Bess the Newfoundland, who
still needed to be relieved of her milk. They licked her
teats with a relish, and as they grew older, became unman-
ageable and were sold to a travelling circus.
I remember the Chickering rosewood piano, the red plush
family album on a marble top walnut table, with the word
Album in metal Spencerian across the cover, and I remember
being obsessed with raising the word at the lower corner of
the letter A.
There was the horsehair furniture, two steel engravings of
Landseer in black frames edged with gold inside, one of
them The Stag at Bay—the other I do not recall—we
still possess the Duke of Wellington milk pitcher in copper
    luster.

259

I am the punctuation to this single sentence, no other to bear
the name—with me it goes out—my loss, my gain—
perhaps—foolish contention.

My father with his two strong wives lies in the family lot
on the banks of the Androscoggin,
he was clean-mouthed, clean-souled, proud of being honest,
avoided being conspicuous in any other way.
The finest people in the world are those who act in the
right way;
My mother and father were among them.

The Bend of the Androscoggin

At Topsham,
winter-swept,
coming up into the picture world
like a Yankee Breughel—the branches
of the trees whitened and
the little group of black termites
skating about the curved spot,
swept for the pleasant occasion;
French Canuck, salt Yankee skating
upon the same geometrical impact
inscribing anesthetic arc to smooth away
the progress of a testy day—
give it something of an average
state of grace.
How well we know this subterfuge,
who push the wind—face monumental gale—
grit teeth to stultify
pernicious interval,
relieve perplexity.

Elias Gove—or, The Second Coming

I well remember Elias Gove, or at least I think I do.

He looked very tall to me when I was a child;
but maybe he wasn't at all—anything looks big when one is little.

I see a tall handsome man with sumptuous
white hair and a beard like a homeles Neptune's;
he wore light grey clothes, a long frock coat,
a tall light grey top hat with a wide grey band on it;
he carried a grey umbrella loosely bound
and maybe the latest novel of the period,
or probably, truth to tell, it was his Bible.

He had a sweet womanly face, soft and deliberate,
with something intense inside it—
I think I never heard his voice, but I saw
the terrible look in his eyes, of something
majestic and divine about to happen.
He said Christ was coming again—"He is set for the second
coming and He will come—woe to the world when
He does, because His beauty is blinding and wonderful"—
and it seems as if the face of Elias became paler and paler,
like a miracle that you wouldn't think would happen.

Elias went away;
I have never thought of asking where he went
but just the other day someone said:
"do you remember Elias Gove—he was crazy you know,
he thought he was God and Christ in one,"
and I said: "yes, why yes, I do remember Elias Gove—
I remember that he talked of the second coming
but as far as I know it never happened, and no one
knows of Elias Gove now—only the thing he said would
happen never did."

He could not stand to see the thing we see,
and how—how do we?

262

Two Drowned at the Gateway

They walk on the waves at night—
all day they sleep beneath;
one wears a lantern on his brow,
one wears a wreath made of quivers of the sun.

One had learned what love is,
had pondered some of its frail mysteries;
and one,
one had not yet learned
how it was to be learned;
nineteen and twenty-two,
lost at the gateway.

The mother looks out of the window
each misery night;
she sees the glow of the lantern on the brow
and hears the quivering of the wreath.
Why do they walk and shine in the night
when they were so beautiful by day?
Says she to each: "O my glimmering boy,
will you not come
where it is warm?
It is cold facing the night,
it is so cold in the night
I am frozen with fright.

"Will you never come to the hearth again,
my gleaming sons
my precious men?
I hear nothing but the moan of the wave
and the windgroan."
When it is darkly dark
she sees the gleam of the lantern,
she hears the quivering of the wreath
again—shadows
these two that yesterday were men,
her own little children.

The Outcast City on the Kennebec

The little city looks as if it had been
washed up by the tides after the islands
had got through with them;
it is now whitening like the thin chips of bone
one sees after life is done,
whatever it was that had one.

Pity
is something you can give an outcast
city
as you can give it to a lady or a gentleman
who have now no calling cards to leave
and so among the shells behind the shutters
they stay
listening to the rain drop slowly from the eaves
and gutters
which give a lot when rains do not forget
to come, and ease the fret.

The little city on the western bank
looks over—Parker's Head they say it is
whispering—well do I remember the time
when we played together—
there was lots of talk between us then
and we exchanged mottoes with each other,
pictures in many colours, blue ribbons,
doves cooing, edged with paper laces
and these were sent to various places—
"Let not our friendship wither like the rose
but like the hemlock and the fir,
forever steadfast be."

It is not nice for little cities
to go and leave us like this—
wanting them back, knowing they
cannot come back—
we like our little cities to keep
their flushed cheeks
and their snappy little ways
but I guess they somehow too get tired

when the bright faces and the climbing muscles
go off and leave them—
"we just couldn't take it any longer"
and they follow the miracle-whirr
of mechanical wing—
"we must really go where there's something doing."

When I saw the crisp bird with warm
feathers clinging to it go down
among the sedges by the shore—
waiting for us to go or look to other ways
and when we didn't she went in anyhow
and stayed,
and we knew that she had found a city
that was not outcast, and that her
children would be rocked to sleep when
she left them for a turn among the seed harvests
on the rugged bank;
we knew she would have a lot to thank, more than us
even though we were so decently curious.

O little outcast city, why did you give in—
you who lived so tenderly in the glow
of the western lantern?
And all the little houses answered in unison:
    "we have perfected our days—
    those who have loved us are gone—
    our ways are no longer their ways—
    something that is done with, and done.
    It is they who have left us, not we
    who have left them, as you can plainly see.
    The proud adventures of the flesh being over
    they have turned rover.
    Something must be done for the mind—
    we cannot stay with decay and the wind."

Six houses are this outcast city
and there's the fainting, and the pity.

Two Lovely Ones

Two lovely ones—aged seventy—
a man and a woman
lament the same song:

Pity the defectives—
we who are left derisively alone,
we who cling like feathered moss
to furrowed, indifferent stone—
curled to a crisp without percipient
imagining won,
thinking that we owned the single
legacy of sun
because it looked so bravely on.
Marked the harried frozen brow—
forgot the cherished, perished vision
that lay drifted solemnly like snow
upon a far-unwonted field,
like relinquished glory upon a
rusted shield.

Pity this thing
with lopped, fluted, flailed wing—
we who sit and see it clutch
to simmering bough—
beak impaled with press of wind—
eye, at dreadful last, to wonder blind—
bird to wave not falling
like its joyous kind
zealously—
breastbone
slit—broken
with intestate thunder
dusty we—
without fevered force to conjure
for what 'tis said will follow
"after"—pathetic plunder
in over-peopled height
or vacant hollow
where lives neither hawk or dove
eagle or swallow
or fervored eremite

or thing perfectly done
exquisitely forgiven.

This glimpse of transitory Eden
crushed like a fold of leaves
beneath some far-consistent cloud,
its very whisper speaking loud—
"let this be your wedding shroud
when you to nothing will be wed,
appropriately married."
This is what the aged to each other said—
examining their vertical, vertiginous distress:
"where is it decent wishes go,
twinged with filaments of exacting dream?
Do they like faith wash to and fro with tides
caught up on some spur of stone
then swayed to some oblique oblivion?

The winter of their eminent distress
bound them tenderly together in
singular duress.

This Little City

This little city in the sea
steeped in the silence of some vast amenity
of wild, perpetual, courageous things—
cast with the bounty of brave commensurate wings
that have each hour of explicit day
enfolded in a swerved embrace
the solace
of commensurate verity—
shoulders mounting everywhere to face
the crest of crude contingency of place—
gift upon the brow of flushed
thanksgiving
that makes even broken lip sing,
conscripted laughter of devout
simplicity
pouring out of their eyes that greet
the ploughing wind
as others proud of the graced returning
of their all but vanished race
give back forespoken tithes of
somehow continuity—
others basking in brisk contrariety of sun—
these the couraged men,
the fishermen.

Islands in Penobscot Bay

Here they sit
in the manner of black notes
upon a metal sheet of music—
sol-fa-mi-re-do—
timed, tempered, toned,
submerged with indigenous sharps.

How often have we seen
such islands—even in
the faces of men and women we know—
as dark winged ducks at evening
who, for no reason at all, become
restless at the edges of their
evening,
as if the downfall of the sun
being perfect
impelled another area for sleep.

Plain birds racing from almost
loquacious skies,
among those smileless branches
of the pine, the fir, the spruce,
the hemlock,
emitting some casual diatonic array,
some casual melody on a theme
that evening comprehends—
tapering off time to silences
empirical.

People crawl into these bird
sanctuaries in the early beaming
of summer,
like beavers into their dams, thinking
themselves immune from secular invasion.
They say that every now and then a
moose appears from the main,
crossing the waters of the bay,
a bay that is just more distant waters.
Perhaps they like the sting of the salt
upon the shins and nostrils—

for even animals covet—as we—
interstitial release—
as we—from all but sinister
functioning.

Islands say, when they are alone
(do they take their speech from us?)
"we are too much like ourselves,
rivers of vision flow by our cliffs and marshes,
now and then a wing dropping a feather,
the loon loving the teardrop of a lake
seen upon cosmic lids.
North birds go to sleep among the
swirling lilies,
then swing out at flush of sudden morning,
and we are left alone,
so like—ourselves."

"An island is something to be discouraged"—
said an aged one—
"it wants itself and hated to give it up"—
sol-fa-mi-re-do
besieged with indigenous sharps.

Fishermen's Last Supper

For wine, they drank the ocean—
for bread, they ate their own despairs;
counsel from the moon was theirs
for thc foolish contention.

Murder is not a pretty thing
yet seas do raucous everything
to make it pretty—
for the foolish or the brave,
a way seas have.

These Six or Several Houses

These six or several houses
slowly bending at the knee
from the general fatigue of being
kind to so many;
begging the elm, the willow, the fir, the pine,
the spruce, the hemlock to shelter them
now that they are old, as they did when they
were young together.
"Be generous with shade," these falling domiciles
cry out— "we need affection from some familiar avenue."
Passing now among them on the banks of the
Kennebec at Martown, with Pippsburg in the
distance among the waters,
I was impressed with their common plight;
how excessively human they seemed.

There Is an Island

There is an island,
and you will see it as we see it living here,
faun turned to reindeer
from a Finland waste,
nibbling at mosses through rifts of
snow, pawing them, sniffing well
the frozen salt,
reading the newspaper at two A.M.
saying, "lovely is the twilight of the north—
lovely is the twlight of the various Penobscot"—
and the Kennebec over there,
smiling gently at its river-mouth
and the sacrosanct persistence of pure youth—
fire in the bone
with shyness at the skin—
left with their amazing acres of green
grass to wander in,
the name stamped upon every rustling
shoulder blade,
full summer girding all adjacent loins
as Christ with frozen lip suspended
speaks of something pitiably contended,
when black birds in a frenzy circle—
dramatizing all.

Robin Hood Cove — Georgetown, Maine

When evening comes to its gentle arias
along the dusky cove,
and the blue heron flies like a slow arrow
along the selvages of the cove,
as if to give its signal for fine music,
and the little birds who have been so warm
all day have gone in among the pine-spills
for their tithe of rest—
the white bridge joining bank to bank of the tidal river
takes the hushed tones of evening to it ingratiatingly;
the gulls having nothing more to say
to each other—fold wings as pure hands are
folded for a silent thought.
I stand with them all in high salute,
saying to myself: "thanks—well done—beautiful things—
I receive my width of grace from you
and am put to rest with evening singing."

A. Lincoln—Odd, or Even

The brow
so far receded now
pathetically strewn
with mystic vision.

"Lincoln"
cannot cover
split bone
but, if it can,
reminds all
of human
consecration.

The face
so filled with manifest
(peculiar zest)
geographies of spirit—
great countries where
soul might wander,
find no stilted habitation
but room
to forget gloom
space to breathe under
branch and leaf
without expensive grief.

To herein look
is to pitch one's tent
with benefit of sacrament
between furrow
hill, valley, smooth
plain
built of sorrow
with incessant cawing of rook,
trust old stars
again—
stars that never break their word,
sing cheap refrain,
insult loves,
cause unholy pain.

Empire
can go no higher,
be born
of no holier fire.

This Portrait of a Seadove—Dead

Seadove in a shroud
of sand, all shiny with
thick clips of sun—
seadove in a shroud
of sand, and the last word
spoke—alone.
I did not carry messages
for love or war, to end their
ways,
I only bore flicked wave caresses
took them to a timely place;
I gave them to my brood to drink,
a draft of silence on the brink
of death I gave, telling them also
to be brave,
have grace
to face
the loneness of their days.
I shut my eye on a kiss
of sun,
and this I give to
everyone.

This Crusty Fragment

This crusty fragment
of windbeat island
for only silence and
wild winds meant,
in my hand—
dark as an eagle's shoulder
or the look of something
terrible and rare
come up for whiffs of air—
battling once with
volcanic insurrection—
lying still,
warming my palm
with late-fallen flares of sun
upon
its mold-hued face.
I like it near me;
I do not fear me
to kiss its jagged cheek
because I am meek
with love of home place.

I have kissed hard lip
of continent;
I have taken it in arm.
But now, where is its charm
when fainting hope
is but blurred gleam of
periscope?

There will be party soon,
chiefly for the young.
They will be dancing at the party,
dancing with their foolish blood
for it is strong. Youth at the flood—
how can it know—
it is so young, so cold,
so old.

There will be bits
of islands broken

as this one in my hand,
unthinkable token
of desperate demand.

The Berry House

The Berry house was burned
last night—
think of it;
and only yesterday Newman
and myself were looking
at it and I remember saying
what a handsome house—if I were
building I would want mine
to be just like the Berry house;
it was so squarish as we looked
and now it is thoroughly baked
and cooked
and the shape of it is slender,
and not nearly as tender.

You could think in a house
like the Berry house
that is, you could think pleasantly
for squarish is always best
for the shape of a house—
some houses are so thin, or short
or cautiously content with being small—
some look as if there wasn't any room at all
but just an open place to let in
summer and try to keep the winter out
they never seem to know quite what
they are about—
so many lives just like that too
like the houses they live in
and will always be.

It was grey, just like so many
never wanted to be painted I guess
and so stayed that way
and they were useful to the last
for things could get in at night
and hide their stealthy measures
shame of ignorance
or be downright happy perchance.

Well, the Berry house is flat now,
when yesterday it was so generously
square
and that is all there is to that.
I saw the photo of a certain Mr. Berry
in a plush album—
my heavens, but he was handsome—
they'll never come like that again
either women or men.
There'll be many blueberry shrubs
next year,
and even that seems queer.

Sea Burial (1941)

Confidence

We'll have the sun now,
the quaking seagulls said—
We've run the gamut of the thundering sea,
one by one—one by one,
and though the wave is full of bread
a wing is often tendon-weary
of a thing so varied-vast—
We do our geodetic surveillance,
for herring are a shining thing,
a shape of sleek imagining,
a pretty circumstance—
The shiver of an ash leaf and of pine
makes other music for a day's determining,
even sea gulls love the shape of roses
ere day closes.

In Robin Hood Cove

The tide comes in, and out goes tide—
it skirts the cliffs, and in their shadow sees
the remnants of the days that fall
between a seagull's and a robin's call.
There is the bridge, and under flows
the rests of evening with its primulous
shows.
It is a river made of listless sea
after it has explained its fierce integrity.
No thunder makes, or on rock heaves,
it learns the place for plain humility,
and keeps reflection of some mindless
leaves.

These evening greens
that gather wistfully among
the ripening coronals of summer
when rain has done its streaming
and the sea has washed back
its waters into these little cities
made of whispered wish
and gentle, seabird thought, homely consecration—
Airs—vibrant with the felt glimmer of a day
gone down to glory of a sunken yesterday;
Night stepping in, soft-shot and separate
in her smooth design;
these evening greens
that gather wistfully, making melody
of nothings in their tuneful
prime.

The lonely Return to the Lonely, the divine to the Divine
— Proclus

Have they not, the lonely, understood those
treasures held in quivering hand, gathered from
the stately hill of hardihood, or shadowed
valley underneath of perhaps, pain—
who, in their singular and profiled difference
repose, within the circled circumstance,
have they not also burned with fervours
of their brooding reticence,
flown too like blown butterfly, brushed with
solar efflorescences, who when love is strictly won,
and the fine offices are done,
swing out to sea, straightly to the north,
serving mariners as compass,
so straight the esoteric sense,
until, like him, they seem to see infinity too near
and tremble for what is much too dear,
that it is a kind of extravagance to be alone
when cool circumference is revealed
by lips having courage to withhold,
believing wisdom is the best when sealed
up, and kept for silent reference.

The lonely—the Divine
are they explicit one
to each,
does each teach its own reach
to other,
that one is shadow, one is gleam—
one the wave length,
one the stream
is not stillness like the breath of living
without wanting
after all the frets are over,
when depth has to the surface told,
its chivalries manifold?

The Man—the Father

Passed by the little fresh water pond
this afternoon on the way from the sea,
stopping, buying new carrots, beets, new peas, new
raspberries fresh from the vines,
and there was a huge man and two little girls who had
finished their bathing and were drying off on the
rocks.
The man's back was turned south, and he was very like a
certain David, wide shouldered, small waist, round buttocks,
iron legs, all muscle and sinew, and the worked look of
his skin told him to be in his first forties.
The girls were young and new looking, for nothing has as
yet touched them, or disturbed the held gleaming of their
childishness, and their breasts were barely formed.
Man faced about breast facing south, and he magnificent,
with smooth dark hair coming to a point on a low forehead, a firm mouth, the upper lip a little short, showing
milkwhite teeth, and the eyes a deepest dark.
His powerful manhood spoke above all whispers over him,
hands and face bronzed with burning of sun, the legs
eggwhite.
He went over to the bushes to undress and redress,
then rejoined the young girls and without question he
was their father, what a father, built in every portion as
a man should be, no feminine curve anywhere, as sometimes
happens in a man—everything right, opulent, tense, forceful,
spreading out his father wings over the scarcely
feathered things beneath him.

Indian Point

When the surf licking with its tongues
these volcanic personal shapes, which we
defining for ourselves as rocks, accept
them as such, at its feverish incoming—
isn't it too, in its way, something like
the plain image of life—
those restless entities disturbing solid
substances with a curious, irrelevant,
common fret—
And, like so many simple looking elements, when
they seem the most playful, it is then that
they are most dangerous.
The bright woman looking out to sea
through the crisp telescope of her advancing
years,
there is no doubt but that she discovers the
same image as the child, who, remarking the
radiant glint of his marbles on the top spray
of the wave he once played with,
or as the fringed lace on the dress of a
titan's wife—
the inwash cooling at least the eye with
a something exceptional white or green or
blue too pale almost to mention, if frightening to the marrow,
for many have been sent to their death trusting too much, while regarding it affectionately,
the sea.

Cyriaque d'Etremont

Bluenose Portrait Effect #1

Battles tucked away in padded cells
to keep brainlobes fervently inflamed
with memory's magnetary push and press
long procession plowing the purple mould
treading measuredly on dreams, awed, stiffened
with cold
over smooth fell and heat shivering plain,
the stout strains abaft sowing seed to
greet good gains of Acadian brawn
hunters hunting for a high-priced dawn
beating the bush to start some fiend from
under,
tie it, split it, break it up into bits,
spew it like carrion morsels to buzzard
gullet
holding tight the untucked schemes of love
crushing love sacred arms and breasts
men dreaming of dynasties as plowing,
raking pools of phosphorescence at each
cup-dip of oar,
and the long thin trail of phosphor at
stern,
bravery tied on like winter cap in winter,
well fastened under the chin to keep cheap
failure out,
and smart winning, in.

Ninety-six years in one house,
CYRIAQUE—
how you must love the very teething of
the woodnit,
grinding gums on joists and keeping them
from trembling at the softness of the
voice,
ninety-six years,
how blood boiled up, cooled itself off,
and was splendid,
eyelashes curved for daredevilling of one
kind or another, tearing bosom buttons to

snare the bloom of seashells,
under
clutch at the sheer nascency of them,
be drugged by their thin-spun opium,
whet the lips at the finger-feel of axeblade,
sharpened for the chip-chip of that brawnfull
fall,
prescient nativism in every sweep and thrall,
faces that forever smile climbing every bedpost,
every wall,
frozen breath of oxen sticking out of nostril,
and nostril
smarting of the frosts that glisten them—
what glyptographs must line the very film of
CYRIAQUE'S brain, as he sits whittling and twining
and intertwining them
stratagem for stratagem
new world magnificent with purloined
old-world thunder
and the spirit's mitred and croziered
plunder.

Blair Purves

Bluenose Portrait Effect #2

Thick-shanked, broad-flanked Purves,
Blair if it's all the same to you—
set out at swift eighteen to do a thing
or two among them, shake a family tree
out of its rawboned lethargy.

The width of his chest and the lay of
his back
shine like a glistening railroad track
over which new trains of passion have begun
to make steep grades and giggle at the sun—
the thick of his lip, hat over one eye—
you know by the slant just why eighteen
is the time to take it, when it makes all the
difference in the world—
thus the rakish slant of the hat,
and can he be blamed for that?

Images like Blair are made for thinking
fast
wondering how long flame and fire will last—
they must be looked at, felt the impress of,
and if he says, feel my biceps—how's that now,
I get 'em from trees, cuttin' 'em, rolling' 'em
into rivers
it is only what something generations past
said—
feel my biceps and thighs, I'm in a hurry,
got a lot to do—they were all that way,
back of me.

Blair says to me—all I want to do
it to split the bull's eye into two—
I hear my tree-rollin' grandpa say
split 'em Blair like I done it, don't forget
now
split 'em in two.
He could handle a gun like the best son

of a gun,
an' I'm his next but one son.

Blair is a bluenose—you can take it
just the way it is.

The shoot is off for another season
if I didn't get it as I want it now,
meaning the gold disc with the red ribbon,
I got another year to shine up in,
that'll be enough to show him how.

He's gone back, Blair Purves, so they say
down Massaquodaboit way,
if that's where he came from, giant-like
or was it Pubnico or Tusket, Jeddore, or
somewhere up beyond the "Arm"—
he'll have his due you may be sure
he'll have his medal on his width of chest
clinking like a sunset on his chest,
and that will tell the blazing rest—
he'll have his medal 'fore he gets a wife
and that he says on his life.
Them you can get at any point in life—
you can tell by the chemical slant of his
hat,
them you can get any moonlight night,
sometimes it's much too quick in the moonlight,
so says the slant of his hat.

If We Could

If we could do what the white birds
do,
break the brink of the wind with blade
of stiff wing,
shatter it to splinters as wave-dash
takes the rocks, shrieking loudly,
O I can take it if you can, almost smiling
and the light smoke-curves from incessant
chimneys
clinging to a cloud that is white,
can afford to be explicitly
erudite.

If we could do what the white birds
do,
measuring every width of sea so non-
chalantly,
take the kick of thunder to our ribs,
politely,
or the upflare of morning with applause,
that would be something by which to
remember us,
who ponder, thus.

You Who Have Done

You who have done with the little
wanderings and finger playings such
quick early love, domestic piety, the
flushed disasters to the flesh and bone,
recovery of what heart needed most,
touch of unprofessional sincerity,
foot that breeds with speed the mile
of quietude,
the moment comes at last, when you can
profoundly say
come sky, come earth, come night and day,
come — cream
let us live together quietly,
you too have opened the clear clean window
of the "quelque chose d'autre," and what is
more than a thousand nights of satisfaction —
CLARITY.

Any Page of Thomas Mann's

Out of the mould from the molten flow
cooled in the mould, the bell the founder's
joy
flawless in its tone, the heart plumbed to the
rim of the world—
the dream caressed like a sheath its warm
dagger,
like a sheaf of fresh birds from the new
spring,
then the harvest garnered—look how what
gleams in the sun—
the arms strong and beautiful, bound round
the gleaming body awaiting masks merged in
a quiet frenzy of something to be heard
across a field at matins or vespers,
head bound and bowed for a moment at that
blossoming of the unexpected smile—
fingers cooled at the tips with almost too
much of assertion
and the lying back in the shadow of a strong
tree
satisfied,
that so much of the substance of things is
ITSELF.

What Is Sacrament

The sea is wild and black and black
a devil curse is in the dark
of the wind,
nothing has strength to be kind
the vague earth would give much of
its very breath
to be free of the clutch of death
even if it go blind.

Gulls go greyer on a stretch of grey.
They have so much to, fainting, say
but cannot speak for terror's majesty
being all but cracked in two with fear
just as people often are.

The sullenness of things is terrible
sabres clash, bombs go spitting out
their welltimed murder,
old women tend their useless knitting,
Ichneumon stings the flesh of decent
things, and infants drop away
their pure hearts pure blood spent,
nothing of itself is sure,
even the unborn are wondering what
is sacrament.

As the Buck Lay Dead

As the buck lay dead, tied to the fender
of a car
coming down from Matagamon way,
I saw the dried blood on his tongue, of
a thousand summer dreams and winter cogitations
the scratches on his hooves were signatures
of the many pungent sticks and branches,
the torn place in his chest was made
by a man
letting out viscerals to save weight-giving
morsels to many a greedy fox or other wild
thing,
over the glaze of his half-shut eye
hung miseries of superlative moments
struck dumb.

Richard Rolle

Sunclad, steel-shod eremite
Richard the blinding-white
Richard the filled-with-light
hunger-fed, God-encountered Richard
he who sought the flaming heart,
Richard the engulfed-with-love
loved the burn, craved the smart,
crowned with singing murmurs of
the Dove.

His home is in a morning cloud
and in his sackcloth-transported
shroud,
he sings his molten migratory hymn,
up to the floating cherubim;
prisms are his sunlost eyes,
and his silences are melodies
which only summer birds may sing
whose hearts are made of morning fire
and skies, the house of their imagining.

Richard sings of the inviolable love
and the pristine burden thereof;
he strums a magic, shimmering lute,
that shall nevermore be mute—
Richard, the clothed-in-white;

YHESU—thou God-grown sweet,
I would be thy sacred intimate.

Horowitz

Those piston-driven fingers at the key-
board like tigers burning bright in the
middle of a cataclysmic rage,
tearing the tones apart as fish-hawks tear,
one claw holding them down, fish-snacks from
fish skeletons,
scattering the bones upon wind-bitten waves.

This sense of being aware at once of everything
in the full-fledged instance, leaving immortality
like a fleck on the face of the sun,
the man himself pulled out of a sheer mirage
leaving him bare of heart,
with stately soul drawn upward by the hair
like some mad thing in a Blake drawing,
only when we LEARN—are we suspended between
crashes of thunder and jabs of lightning
do we know the glory of the single moment
lived,
it is the certainty that we have lived what
the sense contrived outside all metaphysical
flat pauses,
that music like this is made,
giving credence to wisdom's fiercest surmise.

Giant and Saint

In these vast bodies of the stupendous
men and women
that tender spot the soul, offering the
only means we have by which we can be said
to navigate,
from which we get our equilibrium, equanimity,
freedom, sensing the vast in the little
and the little in the vast;
the comic situation of the atom, the
amoeba, the hormone—
the laughter of the hormone coming to the
surface, hitting us in the face and then making
play for air, incidently making fools of us
at dinner, or in the best of company.
The knowing isn't so bad but the lack of
tact on the part of these august institutions
in so-called society makes it difficult to
take it where it lands, which is usually on the teeth
and our much discussed sense of average sainthood
goes skating on thin ice.

Be That as It May (1941)

Midnight — the City

Midnight the city of incredible
contours
tracing out geometries of fleshly
anathemas
and the cool look of flowers under
a strange acre of glass —
not even a moth to corrupt there
childish conducts believing in the
crossword puzzles of eclectic despairs
and the tame delusions of midnight
the city.

Midnight — the city
the irrepressible vertical, raised
to a monolith the size of an Egypt's
or a Doric or a Corinthian
the phallic integer of the personal
pronoun quaffing away, always
short of breath, wheezing at the knees
and a kidney out of kilter in the
end —
no laughter from the midriff
groin, grinding at the little strip
of factual geometry
amid what welter of insidious
deceit.

Old Lady in the Park

With a withered bird hand
leaning out, imploring, as if
saying—
O immortal distance come not
so near,
I know too much of what you
mean,
much more than of what is here.

Lay off my beaten frame.
Let wind take some of the blame
but bring no hand to guide me
I still have pride
in what once seemed reality.

The Ladies and the Pigeons

You hear the gurgling of the bull
pigeon as he struts after the
streamlined little lady who is
intent upon gathering crumbs at
the feet of the human ladies.
It is the action of the bull pigeon
that attracts the ladies who are
finishing up the forties.
There is the look on their battered
faces—of—
I seem to have heard that rumbling
before—
and they return to their casual
chatter.

Fourth Printing

Due to the working success of the
three large editions of himself
he—seeing in retrospect—these
squarely outlined blocks of just plain
experience—
he felt coming by virtue of legitimate
inheritance the fourth aspect of
his consciousness, and because he
knew he had lived through one
moment of pure experience he could say
O Saints, prophets, and fish-mongers
I have lived
and am therefore free to go ahead
with this fourth condition of myself
before taking off for the exquisite
condition of divine nothingness
to which every tired soul is
entitled—
        Yours Sincerely.
        Amen.

P.S. Everyone is entitled to die
on his own fourth large
printing—O Sweet nothingness—
        Yes.

Furnished Rooms

We who confide our dreams
in furnished rooms
find no one to refute them
so much has lived in furnished
rooms
to impute them.

Lives have gone out—
lives have come in—
some with certainty—
some with doubt
who have seen the tempest
and conflagration.

Some Moments with Locatelli

Have we heard morning being broken
into sacred bread before
Have we the right to set lips to these
morsels
when all our teeth are broken with
deception
and the foul hair of well wishers
hanging to the ground, striking terror
to the brows which are their own.

Not that it is not given in music
from the far places of that sky of
the imagination
that does not bring respite in its arms
laying little mercies at our feet
so bruised from the falling
of the stones from the hill
the spirit by itself being grateful.

A Going Man

I watch him, dying an old
fashioned death
who has ever devised a unique
one,
slowly falling asleep in the abused
park of his imagination
the grass no longer green, the moon
muffled to an inveterate grey
the spirit kicked about from pillar
to post
a mendicant no longer wanting
anything.
When he made the sign to me
drawing his slim fingers across
his throat,
I knew what he meant—it is
finished—the gall blistering the
tongue
the foot too tired to step upon
another grain of earth.
Well beautiful man, for whom
I have nothing but love
what more is there to offer
but some little rests of smouldering
sleep
in the abused park of the imagination.

There Is Spit upon the Daisy Stem

There is spit upon the daisy stem
we children used to get our fingers
wet with it—
wiping it off on our clothes.
In the center we would see a small
white worm
with black pinpoint eyes
it looks more foolish than wise.
I never yet learned what took wing
from such a slime
yet we must sensibly assume
something did—
something trivial, though perhaps sublime.

Fabian Bell—His Last Visit to Cuernavaca

No more Fabian, no more like that,
sauntering in the garden made of
sleeping vines and coloured stone.
No more measuring of the oblique meridian.
I saw him walk like jaguar toward
a haze of sky
grey eyes talking in their half-dream
sleep
having words with silver spoons at table
under a smitten pergola,
shading his face from the quick thunders
of the hybiscus umbrages
acres of flayed wonder on his brow
falling to finger tips in slim tensions
deficit so sharply known, so sharply
known.

Never a smile like Fabian's, as if
stolen from the mouth of a child,
flowering then once again without stem
or root or leaf.
Blithe Fabian, temples streaked with
first fall of snow
speaking small elegies to sudden birds
that spring from out the mango boughs
dropped songs from Inca scenes
fluted for the earth in time of such
perplexities
Fabian, now dead—
a certain space will always name
his name.

Five Women

These five, stepping to the scythes
saying
here you men, give us the blades
sharpen them if you like—but we'll
do the field
there's plenty of time before sundown.

You should have seen the five,
swinging the blades across the blazing
wheat—
beauty is in strength said they.
Why are the men so weak?

The men lay under the trees
sleeping
resting from their women—
when they awoke the fields
were sheaved.
Our women are wonderful
the wheat is done
we shall have bread.

Metaphysic

If it were not for the charm of
crossing so many borders, we would
all be dead from the fatigue of not
crossing them.
We struggle to get away from the shackles
of something that wasn't us, or from the
romantic pressure of something that says
let us go to other places and be ourselves
in them, or else better still, be something
we do not know we could be, in
them.
Space opens the gateways of [our]
determined sense to remain the
same thing.

Time says you come with me.
I will show you the reality of every
dream you had the strength to conjure—
and still we loll about tying false
shoe-strings, eating bread that has nothing
in it but itself, the wheat all blown
to the birds, the husks baked in
the nearest oven, and we, famished with
another hunger than we have yet known
thirsting for a wine that only rainbows
have closed their eyelids on
amazed at our strangeness to—ourselves.

Three Friends

Outline for a Picture

These three men are friends.
The central figure is of course—
Christ,
because he has suffered the most—
suffered through suffering—and
therefore has risen above it.
Christ has come down off the
cross
and is seated at the base of it
dwelling upon the meaning of pain
rather than the experience of it.

The second friend—
kneeling at the left is the
prizefighter,
he has suffered plenty but for
a foolish idea
and so his body is hurt all the
more with it—
and so he prays on his knees
for deliverance from the foolish
idea.

The third friend
at the right is the clown
who having suffered almost
as much as Christ—or thinks
he has—
spends his energies in the perfection
of comedy and grotesquerie—
and, having learned the divine secret
of laughter
proceeds to perfect himself in the
knowledge of laughter.

Who is the fool among them—
is it perhaps the gentleman
with the fine face—
in the Center?

and is being the perfect fool
as great an achievement
as any other?

When we have learned
exactly this—
we shall all be perfectly
wise.

Patterns for Prayers (ca. 1940–43)
For One who could not pray

> "I may speak of that which
> I know by experience, and so I
> say—let him never come from
> prayer who has ever begun it,
> be his life ever so wicked.
> For prayer is the way to renew
> it and without prayer such
> amendment will be much more
> difficult."
> St. Theresa of Avila,
> *Autobiography*, chapter 8

The Lost, Alone

It will be honorable to pity
him. This one—
who having given up his blood
to little things, the shimmers and
the sheen of impecunious intimations
now left upon the river bank, like
a morsel of wood swept down stream
then caught and held by a jutting rock
to permanently feel the shock.

I listen to his talk and feel leaves falling
round my head—
leaves that once were green and loved
the rush of chlorophyll along their veins
these leaves that once took shafts of
sun
and made lush wonder of them—
now falling, falling, falling—like snow
upon some Tuesday afternoon in winter
coming to ground to be held a little while

then melt to whispered coagulating rain
upon a pavement thick with pain.

I hear him talk of butterflies, or of
flash of moon light upon a pharaoh's
tomb
the sun covering its earthly tracks beyond
when Monday and Tuesday were at
the cusp,
and the other several afternoons
played round with vigorous [*illegible word*]
upon a single theme.
I could see the Bobi birds circling down
among the stunted balsams and firs
in search of morsels left over from
lumberjacks' luncheons, who never
neglect them because those who [know]
say that in every Bobi bird lives
the soul of a dead lumberman's and they
will not refuse to feed them.

The Nameless Speaks

Lift up Thy little lips
to me again
Sweet child—
O breath of dew before the dawn
upon these baby lips
assuage my pain—
I am all but heart-broken
yet still must face the dreadful
day, again.
Child, kiss me once more
that I may learn to restore
faith—in men.

■

Look down ever-intimate one
see the bird of these ultimate and
inevitable wishes
cries out from its crucifixion
in the sky—
the wind is in its wings, yet
it cannot fly—
break bread a little for its soon
release
it so longs for iridescent peace.
Be sure it will gloriously sing
if ever it be free and strong.

■

Lay warm gentle hand upon me
O Sire—
Let me feel the sacred fire
that shall make me whole
through equanimity of soul.
Lift me out of myself—higher
O higher take me.
Wrap wings about me—let me
feel the stir
of your perfect opulence—bring me
unalloyed desire
and this alone shall make me
Whole
O Sire!

■

O lift me—majestic Sire
touch me with your quenchless
fire.
Keep me—O keep me from falling
down—down into the incredible
abyss
of human helplessness.
Lend me one ray from the
inexhaustible sun
of your immeasurable love.
I would, like the gentle dove
fly to some aspect of your
most generous heaven
and there be saved from dire
oblivion.

■

The day is dark—the night
so blackened with deceit
O Sire.
Help me keep my faltering feet
upon the dear bright road of
heartening peace.
I crave illustrious release,
I yearn for the sacred light
of the morning Sun
to envelop me and make me
one
with all there is, which all
is Thee
in blessed eternity.

■

O where have I wandered—out
of darkness—into dark—you
untouchable One, put finger
on my stinging smart.
Someday I pray to see your face
for it will have I know pure
trace
of human intimation.
It will have I know, the gift
of splendid pity traced thereon,
it will have sweet magnanimity
of the sun,
it will shine like the flesh of
flowers singing in unison,
it will have the dreams of
shimmering birds
made audible—
and these shall be your
sacred words.

■

Do nothing to injure the living
aspect of the human spirit.
It is the only aspect of ourselves
that can afford to live.
The struggle to keep this alive
is our present and painful
predicament.
How can we live, otherwise.

Appendix

The Business of Poetry

1919

I AM RIDING through Arizona in the Pullman. I am thinking of the business of poetry. Every other man attends to the details of business, if he is a good business man. A train is mostly business men. . . .

Poets must, it seems to me, learn how to use a great many words before they can know how to use a few skilfully. Journalistic verbiage is not fluency. Alfred Kreymborg agrees with me that poets do not write prose often enough. I speak mostly of the poets who do not write with the sense of volume in their brevities. Brevity of all things demands intensity, or better say tensity. Tensity comes from experience. The poet must see the space for the word, and then see to it the word occupies it. It is almost mechanical science these days, it would seem—the fitting of parts together so the whole produces a consistent continuity. Subjects never matter, excepting when they are too conspicuously autobiographical. "Moi-même, quand même" is attractive enough, but there are so many attractive ways of presenting it. Personal handling counts for more than personal confessions. We can even learn to use hackneyed words, like "rose" and "lily," relieving them of Swinburnian encrustations. We can relieve imagery from this banality.

Poets cannot, as aspiring poets, depend, it seems to me, ever upon the possible natural "flow" that exists in themselves. Poets have work to do for the precision of simplicity, and for the gift of volume in simplicity. It is the business of good poetry to show natural skill as well as natural impetus. Some poets would like to say the former is more important. It surprises one a deal how much even the better poets effuse, or rely upon their momentary

315

theories. The subject calls for handling, not for enthusiasms. Painters of this time have learned this; or ought to have learned it by now, with the excellent examples of the time. Personality is a state, it is not the consummate virtue. It begins, but it does not finish anything. We have eventually to insert in the middle spaces all we can of real ability. What is much needed is solidity, even of sentiment, combined with efficacy of form. This might be served as an injunction to some of the "girl" poets. Poets have not so much to invent themselves as to create themselves, and creation is of course a process of development.

We are to remember that Ingres, with his impeccable line, was otherwise almost nothing else but silhouette. We cannot subsist merely upon silhouette in poetry, nor upon the pantomimic gesture only. For every lightness there must be a conscious structure. Watteau was the genius of lightness in gesture. No one will accuse him, or even his pupils, Lancret or Pater, of emptiness. A fan has structure by which it exists, a structure that calls for delicate artistry in mechanics. The aeroplane is propelled by motors weighing tons, made of solid metals; and is directed by a master mechanic. Its own notion of lightness would never get it off the ground. Poetry will never "fly" on the notion of its mere lightness, for lightness is not triviality. Francis Thompson had a wing in his brain, but he had feet also. Those men were not mere personalities. They were master mechanics in the business of poetry. A bird could never rely upon the single strong feather. Poetry might rather well take up the mania of Flaubert, if only as a stimulus to exactitude of feeling and idea. You find the best poets doing all they can of that, or else intending that.

The fierce or fiery spaciousness is the quality we look for in a real poem, and coupled with that the requisite iron work according to the personal tastes of the poet. The mere gliding of musical sequences is not sufficient. Poetry is not essentially or necessarily just vocalism. It may have plot or it may be plotless—that is for the poet to decide: what is wanted is some show of mechanistic precision such as the poet can devise. He must know his motive as well as himself, and to invent the process of self-creation is no little task. That is the first principle to be learned by the versifiers. Poetry is not only a tool for the graving of the emotions; nor is it an ivory trinket. It calls for an arm. We need not be afraid of muscularity or even of "brutality."

It is a refreshing omen that big poets write but little poetized autobiography. We find it so much in small poetry, poetry written behind moral arras, where the writer looks out upon a clear space with longing. Anyone would best set it aside, and get outside himself and among the greater trivialities. Preoccupation, blocked introspection, are old-fashioned stimuli for modern poetry. Painting has become definitely masculine at last, in its substance, mechanistic in its purport. Delicacy and frankness are not necessarily feminine. Nor are strength and vigor necessarily muscular qualities. What Mr. Untermeyer pleases to call the "cult of brutality" does not apply to the poets he names, unless he regards all poetry as delicate and "good."* You may find the most infinite tenderness in Masters, in Wallace Gould, and in the others whom he names. He chooses to call picturing brutality. Brutality exists only in the preferential attitude. No one finds Whitman brutal. One finds him presenting the picture. Yet the effect of Whitman on the "sick soul," as William James calls it, is essentially a brutal one. His simple frankness hurts. He removes the loin-cloth because it always hints at secrecy and cheap morality. He undresses the body we are forever dressing. He thinks it handsomest so. He is right. It is a poor body that doesn't look best without clothes. Nature is naked, and, not to speak tritely, quite unashamed. It has no moralistic attitude. It has no attitude at all. It is therefore natural.

*Hartley is probably referring here to Untermeyer's book, *The New Era in American Poetry* (New York: Henry Holt and Company, 1919).

Frost writes of New England, and the natives say they know nothing of that New England. The native who looks in from the outside with a world vision says, "How familiar!" He doesn't say, "How cold, how forbidding!" Masters would probably not wish to live by his *Spoon River*, yet his later books are just other shades of the same powerful grey. Wallace Gould will not want to live by his "so dreadful" *Out of Season*, in *Children of the Sun*; yet his books will probably always be tense and severe. Wallace Stevens thinks, or at least says, he isn't interested in producing a book at all. Well, that is superbly encouraging. It is not therefore what the poet thinks of, that is the "delicacy" of his subject. He is looking for the mechanism by which to render "subject" with the precision called for by his feelings and attitudes toward it.

I personally would call for more humor in poetry. If it is true with poetry as with the play, that almost anyone can write a drama or a tragedy, while the comedy man is rare, this would at least account for the lack of charming humor in verse. Satire is delectable, as Henry James has shown. Even the so serious-minded Emily Dickinson had her inimitable gift of humor. She did the best kind of fooling with "God." An intellectual playfulness with great issues she certainly had to an irresistible degree.

A quotation from someone, apropos of Rainer Maria Rilke, stating that "The poet, in order to depict life, must take no part in it," offers a fine truism. He is of necessity the looker-on. How else? He must see first and feel afterward, or perhaps not feel at all. Modern expression teaches that most noticeably. Real art comes from the brain, as we know, not from the soul. We have the excellent examples of this in Mary Garden and Mrs. Fiske—fine refutations of the attitude toward femininity. It is a geometric of self-invention art purposes to create. The poet, it seems, must learn this along with the other artists of the time. Art of the time is the art of the mechanism of the time. We must make poetry of today according to the theme of radio-telephony, and of commutation over oceans by the plane. We cannot feel as we do and attempt Keats' simplicities, or Keats' lyricism even. We have other virtues and defects. We are not melodists. Cacophonists, then? We do not concentrate on the assonant major alone. We find the entire range of dissonance valuable as well as attractive. Or is it all a fierce original harmonic we are trying to achieve?

There is no less need of organization even if we do not employ the established metre and rhyme. Likewise, if a poet must state his or her personal history, he or she may be asked to be as brief as possible. It is easier to read epigrams than to read the diary, no matter how short the latter may be. The age of confession perished with the Parnassians. We are a vastly other type of soul — if we are soul at all, which I keenly doubt. The poet's attitude then, for today, is toward the outside. This does not necessarily imply surface. We present ourselves in spite of ourselves. We are most original when we are most like life. Life is the natural thing. Interpretation is the factitious. Nature is always variable. To have an eye with brain in it — that is, or rather would be, the poetic millennium. We are not moonlit strummers now: we are gun-pointers and sky-climbers.

Notes

List of Abbreviations used in the Notes

MS   Manuscript (MSS: manuscripts)

MH   Marsden Hartley

MHMC   Marsden Hartley Memorial Collection, Helen and George Ladd Library, Manuscript Collection, Bates College, Lewiston, Maine

YCAL   Yale Collection of American Literature, Beinecke Rare Book and Manuscript Library, Yale University. MSS from YCAL are sometimes identified further by archive listing such as (Berger 15) or (Wells 16)

EP   *Eight Poems and One Essay* by Marsden Hartley (Treat Gallery, Bates College, Lewiston, Maine: 1976)

SP   *Selected Poems* by Marsden Hartley, ed. Henry Wells (New York: Viking Press: 1945)

OA   *Others for 1919: An Anthology of the New Verse*, ed. Alfred Kreymborg (New York: Nicholas L. Brown, 1919)

TP   *Twenty-five Poems* by Marsden Hartley (Paris: Contact Editions, 1923)

AIA   *Adventures in the Arts* by Marsden Hartley (New York: Boni and Liveright, 1921)

SB   *Sea Burial* by Marsden Hartley (Portland, Maine: Leon Tebbetts Editions, 1941)

Early Poems (1904–1918)

In the first four of these early poems, all previously published, some punctuation and capitalization from the printed versions have been changed according to my reading of the holograph MSS.

LIGHT OF NIGHT   First published in EP, pp. 11–13. Text source: holograph MS in MHMC.

NATURE   First published in EP, pp. 18–19. Text source: holograph MS in MHMC. Stanza 4, line 2, the holograph clearly reads "proon" but the word is unknown, and he undoubtedly meant "preen."

THE ROYAL LOVE CHILD   First published in EP, pp. 11–13. Text source: holograph MS in MHMC. Inscribed: "Edmund Hartley Center Lovell, Maine June 1904"—the name he was christened with; after a time he began to sign his paintings and poems (like "Summer Evening" below) "Edmund Marsden Hartley"—Marsden being the maiden name of his stepmother; finally he dropped Edmund altogether.

SUMMER EVENING   First published in EP, p. 23. Text source: holograph original in MHMC. The poem is dedicated "To my niece, Norma Gertrude Berger" and signed "Edmund Marsden Hartley." Another copy of the poem was included in a letter to his young niece, dated April, 1904 (YCAL). Norma Berger remained one of his closest relatives. They maintained a lifelong correspondence, and she typed many of his manuscripts, both before and after his death. Eventually she became the literary executrix of the MH estate. She gave most of his manuscripts to YCAL, while she and the other heirs of his estate gave a number of papers, Hartley's books, two paintings, a series of drawings, and a collection of memorabilia to MHMC.

THE MYSTICAL FOREST   Unpublished. The only extant copy of this poem appears to have been in the possession of MH's friend, Carl Sprinchorn, who gave copies to Henry Wells (editor of SP) in 1945 and to Robert Burlingame in 1951 when they were preparing their respective works on MH's poetry. (See Robert Burlingame, *Marsden Hartley: A Study of His Life and Creative Achievement*, Brown University, 1953, Ph.D. dissertation.) However, no copy was among the Sprinchorn papers given to YCAL. The present text is a compilation of the Burlingame and Wells versions, each of which was missing a line. Burlingame stanza 13, missing line 17, "That inundated the livid orchid with glory," and Wells stanza 11, missing line 4, "He was as light as a sun ray reflected from a mirror dancing." The copy was apparently given to Sprinchorn around 1918 or 1919 when MH visited him in California and gave a poetry reading; but the poem was probably written somewhat earlier, around 1916–17.

The poem resounds with the poetic fervor of Francis Thompson's "Hound of Heaven"—a poem MH knew well. In his essay "Francis Thompson" (AIA, pp. 215–20), MH lamented the passing of the kind of poetry Thompson wrote: "The last Rhapsodist was Francis Thompson, and in the sense of lyrical fervour, the last great poet was Francis Thompson."

CANTICLE FOR OCTOBER First published in *Contact*, no. 3 (April 1921), 11–12. There is a typed copy in YCAL (Berger 2), but it is uncharacteristic of MH's typescripts and may not be original; therefore the text source used here is the *Contact* version. Stanza 2, line 2, "emminent" corrected to "eminent." The poem may have been inspired by a picnic of the Scotch Caledonian clan which MH attended in Boston in late July 1920. In a letter to Stieglitz he noted how "thrilling to hear the beat of the Scotch heart thru centuries in the notes of the pipes and drums" (letter to Stieglitz, August 2, 1920, YCAL).

Ironies out of St. George's (1916–18)

After a wild summer in 1916 in Provincetown with, among others, Carl Sprinchorn, Charles Demuth, John Reed and Eugene O'Neill, MH arranged for inexpensive accommodations for him and Demuth in Bermuda. The island was almost deserted of tourists due to the wartime mining of the harbors, and he was able to paint and write poetry in relative tranquility, remaining there through the winter, until May, 1917.

MH explains the origin of these poems in the following preface to the collection which he wrote when he revised it some years later, possibly (according to Burlingame) as late as 1930. The preface takes the form of a letter to Carl Sprinchorn, to whom the collection is dedicated:

Dear Carl.

Putting things down is one thing, but putting them down for someone [else] is another, and I feel I must have put these verses for you, since I am certain you are the one who will best care for them.

Our friendship was well established and on the way then, beginning more or less around the period when I was in St. George's, Bermuda — and heard the soldiers tell the substance of these pictures, having been sent over for recuperation or light service, and they were naturally full of terrible adventure — Yorkshire men chiefly, and as it was not far from the Yorkshire border in Lancashire that the roots of my own life took their nourishment, I was familiar not only with the type these men represented, but their spiritual and labal [sic] accent as well.

It was hard times for the boy[s] then, and a whole literature especially in the poetical world has come to light from the hearts and minds of those who survived and were accorded gifts to express these experiences.

And as for the men who live, and who are wheeled off, led about by patronizing hands, wards and drudges of charity, and will remain so until fate relieves them of this embarrassment, little or nothing is heard, and nothing much from them. It is kind that they feel the nobility of silence, ageing along as they are, just "messes of mortals" with the faith in the living dream destroyed.

You have since then visited this pretty island yourself and know the charm of it, and you heard nothing of what is in these pages for the boys that are there now were infants then, and if you talked with them, they were aware only that the world is an enchanted place, and this island one of its most favored in enchantment, and if the older men are still there, any of them, tragedies of the past will make no impression.

I have kept these note-pages which were written in pencil until now, thinking they might be worth holding. They have drifted round the world with me since then, lost for years in the welter of possessions one drags about with one because there seems to be always a sense of life about them.

Having then found their sense of direction, which is yourself, I give them to you. Keep them, and if no one else sees them, it will not matter, as they have found the true audience of one.

This passage out of D. H. Lawrence expresses much of the meaning of a man's life, any man's life, and is to be found at the end of the chapter of "The Marriage of Quetzlcoatl" in *The Plumed Serpent*, and when Lawrence is poetically rhapsodic he is likely to be at his best, or perhaps he is always that, and I am one who thinks this writer a better potential poet than he is an arrived novelist.

> And the star that is between all men and all women, and between all the children of men, shall not be betrayed.
> Whosoever betrays another man, betrays [a man] like himself, a fragment. For if there is no star between a man and a man, or even a man and a wife, there is nothing. But whosoever betrays the star that is between him and another man, betrays all, and all is lost to the traitor.
> Where there is no star, and no abiding place, nothing is, so nothing can be lost.

We have our star these many years, you and I, have we not?

The original MSS of the *Ironies* (YCAL, Berger 37) are written on very small grey notepaper in pencil, which (as mentioned by MH in the preface) he had carried around for many years before revising into a typescript (also in YCAL, Berger 7). The original holograph MS contains twenty-five poems, two of which (#9 "I am an Island" and #25 "She had a way of doing") were omitted from the typescript.

In 1918 MH submitted six of the *Ironies* to *Poetry* magazine. Editor Harriet Monroe chose three (none of those published here) and they appeared (along with three other poems—see below) in *Poetry*, 12 (July 1918), 195–201, under the title "After Battle," designated by Monroe over MH's strenuous objections. His typescript for the six submissions, complete with Monroe's editorial emendations, is preserved in the Special Collections at the University of Chicago Library and is important since it includes two poems from the series ("I don't know where" and "They are not much") which are not in the original holograph MS nor the YCAL typescript. In several letters to Monroe, MH requested that the poems not be changed, but she persisted. Her pencilled alterations include the addition of punctuation—quotation marks, exclamation marks, periods and commas—where MH had used (characteristically) only a single dash, comma or period.

"We are knitting now," "Just one more," and "Where should we go" were published with several others in SP, pp. 76–82, under MH's original title. As mentioned in the Introduction, Henry Wells made editorial changes of MH's idiosyncratic spelling, punctuation and capitalization; these changes have been restored according to either MH's typescript or holograph original.

325

SHEPHERD OF THE MORNING   Unpublished. Text source: MH's typescript.

I AM AN ISLAND   Unpublished. Text source: holograph original. Not included by MH in his typescript.

SHE HAD A WAY OF DOING   Unpublished. Text source: holograph original. Not included by MH in his typescript.

LIKE ICE HIS BLOOD   Unpublished. Text source: MH's typescript.

WE ARE KNITTING NOW   First published in SP, pp. 80–81. Text source: MH's typescript. "joseph-hues" corrects "Joseph-hues" in SP version, according to MH's idiosyncratic habit of using lowercase for the adjectival form of a proper name.

JUST ONE MORE   First published in SP, p. 82. Text source: MH's typescript.

WHERE SHOULD WE GO   First published in SP, p. 81. Text source: MH's typescript.

RED TARGETS BLOWING   Unpublished. Text source: MH's typescript. Submitted to *Poetry* but rejected.

BLANDLY SHE LIES   Unpublished. Text source: MH's typescript.

KALEIDOSCOPE (1918–1919)

The original MS of *Kaleidoscope* has not survived. Whether the six *Ironies out of St. George's* poems MH submitted to Harriet Monroe in 1918, formed part of the *Kaleidoscope* collection is not clear. Alfred Kreymborg (who later published several *Kaleidoscope* poems in *Others*, 1919, see below for details), wrote a letter of introduction for MH to Harriet Monroe, stating that several of the poems had been accepted by *The Seven Arts* before it folded. (See letter from Kreymborg to Monroe, March 6, 1918, University of Chicago, Special Collections.) Again MH protested unsuccessfully against changes which Monroe made in his MS. Since, however, in this case we have no original MSS to go by, and

MH's letter does not specify corrections, we cannot determine precisely what those editorial corrections were. We can only speculate from the types of alterations on the *Ironies* submissions, that the numerous exclamation and quotation marks are probably Monroe's additions. Therefore the text sources used here are the published versions as noted below for each poem.

IN THE FRAIL WOOD, HER DAUGHTER, SPINSTERS These three poems, along with the three poems called "After Battle," were first published in *Poetry*, 12 (July 1918), 195–199 and constituted MH's professional debut as a poet.

SWALLOWS First published in *Others*, 5:4 (March 1919), 14.

LOCAL BOYS AND GIRLS SMALL TOWN STUFF First published in, and text source: OA, p. 61, except that in the OA version this poem was followed by one called "Prometheus Fire," the title of which was inadvertently omitted, so that it erroneously appears to be the final stanza of "Local Boys and Girls." When the poem was collected in TP, p. 11, the title was misprinted in lower case, so that it appears to be part of the previous poem, "Above the Level—Gloucester."

SALUTATIONS TO A MOUSE First published in, and text source: OA, p. 62.

FISHMONGER First published in, and text source: OA, p. 65.

THE FLATTERERS First published in, and text source: OA, pp. 65–67. The subject matter indicates that Hartley was still working on the *Kaleidoscope* poems during his months in the southwest (Summer 1918 through November 1919).

SUNLIGHT PERSUASIONS (1918–1919)

As with the *Kaleidoscope* collection, we have no way of knowing if the seven poems published in *Poetry*, 16 (May 1920), 59–69, under the title *Sunlight Persuasions* are only part of a larger group of poems, since no original MS exists. Five of the original seven are included here.

SATURDAY, THE TOPAZ OF THE SIXTIES, TO C——, and THE ASSES' OUT-HOUSE   Text source: *Poetry* version.

THE FESTIVAL OF THE CORN   Later reprinted in *The Turquoise Trail: An Anthology of New Mexico Poetry,* ed. Alice Corbin Henderson (Boston and New York: Houghton Mifflin Company, 1928), pp. 44–51. The *Poetry* version employs a stanzaic structure with multiple indentations. In Corbin's anthology the structure was simplified to a block stanzaic form with minimal indentation. Whether this was MH's revision or an editor's change is not known, but the *Poetry* version more effectively captures the rhythmic staccato of the Indian drum beats and repetitive refrain and thus was selected as the text source for the present edition.

The poem is based on the Santo Domingo Corn Dance which MH witnessed during his stay in New Mexico (1918–19). Native American Indian art first appeared as a subject in his paintings in 1914 while he was in Germany. Indian road shows, artifacts, and culture were immensely popular in Europe during that prewar period, and MH—along with many of his European artist colleagues—frequented Berlin's Ethnographical Museum and Paris's Trocadero Museum where large collections of American Indian art had been gathered. Like "The Festival of the Corn" many of MH's paintings from the New Mexico period are filled with a rich mixture of Indian and Spanish (Catholic) imagery, although the theme of the Corn Dance itself is not a subject in the paintings. (See also the series of prose essays on Indian esthetics which MH wrote at this time: "The Red Man" in AIA, pp. 13–29, and the two-part piece, "The Scientific Esthetic of the Red Man," *Art and Archaeology,* part I, "The Great Corn Ceremony at Santo Domingo," 13 (March 1922), 113–119; and part II "The Fiesta of San Geronimo at Taos," 14 (September 1922), 137–139.

TWENTY-FIVE POEMS (1923)

This first book collection of MH's poetry was published by his friend Robert McAlmon. He and McAlmon first met in California in 1919. Later in New York, MH introduced the young aviator-poet to William Carlos Williams, and the three of them collaborated in producing the first issue of *Contact.*

Originally TP was to have been printed by Charles Boni, who

had published AIA in 1921, but Boni bowed out, apparently for economic reasons. Like most of the early Contact Editions publications, TP received limited distribution—mostly to the poet's friends, a few critics and friendly publishers, and a scant number of bookstores, like Sylvia Beach's Shakespeare & Company in Paris. Likewise the book received only a few reviews, prominent among them being Harriet Monroe, *Poetry*, 23 (November 1923), 105–107.

No original manuscripts for any of the poems exist; the texts used here are based on either the TP versions or some other printed version, details of which are noted below. In the TP versions, commas and periods were inconsistently placed outside quotation marks; these have been made to conform to Hartley's more common usage—inside quotation marks.

WORLD-PASSPORT VISA   First published in TP, pp. 1–2, and later in SP, pp. 55–56, where lines 21 and 22 were omitted, "consistently evolved / for purposes intended"; and line 28 incorrectly reads "to" instead of "in an untoward hour." Text source: TP version.

THE FORK OF ANNIE   First published in, and text source: TP, pp. 8–9.

ARE YOU THERE, ROSE TRUMBULL?   First published in, and text source: TP, pp. 13–14; text corrections in brackets.

GULLS AT GLOUCESTER   First published in, and text source: TP, pp. 14–15.

COBWEBS AND RATHOLES   First published in, and text source: TP, pp. 15–16. This poem, as well as "The Fork of Annie" and "Spinsters," recalls MH's series of paintings on the theme of the deserted New England farm which he executed in 1909–10 at a time when he felt most poignantly the suffocating, effete influence of living in his native Maine. It was soon after this time that he left for Europe, not to live in Maine again for nearly two decades.

BOSTON PORTRAIT PROJECTIONS   In TP there were six poems in this series, three of which were chosen for this edition.

CORILLYN IS DARK   First published in, and text source: TP, pp. 31–33.

RAPTURE   First published in the inaugural issue of *Contact*, no. 1 (December 1920), 9, edited by William Carlos Williams and Robert McAlmon, where it appeared as a one paragraph prose-poem. In TP (the version used here as the text source) Hartley divided the poem into three paragraphs or stanzas and grouped it with the "Boston Portrait Projections," pp. 3–4. Line 4 "is" corrected, according to the *Contact* version, to "Is" and line 14 "Minds" corrected to "minds".

THIS LADY RIDES A LANGUID DROMEDARY TOWARD HER DEAR—GOD   First published in, and text source: TP, pp. 35–37.

DIABOLO   First published in, and text source: TP version, pp. 42–47. In 1920 MH became involved with the newly formed Société Anonyme, hoping that he might be appointed foreign correspondent and be sent to Europe; instead he was made secretary. The group had been founded by Katherine Dreier, Marcel Duchamp and Man Ray to promote modern art through exhibitions, readings, and lectures, and under that stimulus MH wrote DIABOLO and read it before the Society the same year. True to Dadaist performance practices, he included instructions for its reading. See also his essay "The Importance of Being 'Dada'" in AIA, pp. 247–54. MH's involvement with Dadaist artistic methods was, however, peripheral and shortlived.

THE CRUCIFIXION OF NOEL   First published in *The Dial*, 80 (April 1921), 378–80; later in TP, pp. 2–5; and later in *Lyric America: An Anthology of American Poetry*, ed. Alfred Kreymborg (New York: Coward-McCann, Inc., 1930; revised edition New York: Tudor Publishing Company, 1925, pp. 460–62). Minor variations occur in the three versions. The TP version is followed here, except that stanza 10, line 3 omits "hill" erroneously inserted in the TP version. MH first mentions this poem in a letter to Alfred Stieglitz dated March 13, 1920 in which he stated that he would read the poem at the Sunwise Turn Bookstore in April of that year. And later, in 1926, he reminisced to Stieglitz about the origins of the poem which occurred when he had seen an "ultra-modern Xmas tree of only white branches/silicone/moss and blue hanging ornaments" which "blew up into that queer poem" (letters to Stieglitz March 31, 1920 and December 8, 1926, YCAL).

BACH FOR BREAKFAST (1923-1929)

Some of the poems in this collection appear to date from as early as 1923—soon after publication of TP. MH mentioned the collection by name in a letter to Adelaide Kuntz, dated August 23, 1929, describing them as written in a plain rhythm with somewhat of a prose meter and "chant-like tone." Typical of his casual, almost solipsistic attitude toward his poetry, he added that he did not write poetry "for any pressing publication urgency but because it is good for inner health to get these things out" (letter to Adelaide Kuntz, Archives of American Art). The collection is dedicated to an unidentified person: "To van Hasselt Sibriani, recalling super-vistas in Provence" followed by a "corollary" from Spinoza's *The Strength of Emotions*: "Hence it follows that man is always necessarily liable to passions, that he always follows the common order of nature, and obeys it, and that he accommodates himself to it as much as the nature of things demands." The thematic content of the poems in *Bach for Breakfast* concerns his years abroad during the decade of the 1920s: the places he lived—particularly Aix and other cities in Provence; his affection for Paris, his artistic aims as a painter; his isolation (see especially, "The eagle wants no friends"); and the struggles he underwent to eschew what he saw as obsessive subjectivity and the need to find clarification in both poetry and painting. (See Introduction and *Varied Patterns* essays in *On Art*.)

Publication and text source: a collection of thirty poems in typescript with a few alterations in MH's hand; no extant holograph for any of the poems. Four of these poems were published, as noted below; the rest are unpublished and follow MH's typescript.

FROM A PARIS WINDOW—HIGH   First published in *American Caravan*, 4, ed. Alfred Kreymborg, Lewis Mumford, Paul Rosenfeld (New York: The Macaulay Company, 1931), p. 445.

THE WOMAN DISTORTS, WITH HUNGER   First published in *Contact Collection of Contemporary Writers* (Paris: Contact Editions, Three Mountains Press, 1925), pp. 87–90.

TOMORROW BEING MONDAY   Line 32 "Igorot" corrects Hartley's misspelling, "iggerote."

THE BEAUTIFUL RUSH   First published without a title in *American Caravan*, 4 (1931), 447.

LIFE AHEAD, LIFE BEHIND   First published without a title in *American Caravan*, 4 (1931), 446–47.

BEING NEW INSIDE   Line 12 "Zubaran" corrects MH's misspelling "Zuburan."

PROVENÇAL PRELUDES (ca. 1925–1929)

MH lived in several places in Provence during the years 1925 to 1929, when these poems must have been written. Though they parallel somewhat the *Bach for Breakfast* poems in time, place and, occasionally, theme, these Preludes refer strictly to Provence and the characteristic features of that geographic region of France: its "dusty olive trees," the mistral, and the barren rocks.

Publication and text source: a collection of thirteen poems in typescript with minor alterations in Hartley's hand; no extant holographs for any of the poems. Only one poem from this group was published, as noted below, with no discrepancies from the original typescript; the rest follow MH's typescript.

CORNICHE–MARSEILLE   First published in *American Caravan*, 4 (1931), 447.

CITY SCENES (1930–1935)

This group of poems draws from four of MH's compilations from the early and mid-1930s: *Tompkins Square Tabloids* (1931; six poems in typescript); *Fifty-ninth Street Fables* (seven poems in typescript); *City Vignettes* (nine poems in typescript); and *Gay World* (thirty-six poems in typescript)—all of which deal thematically with city life, most notably New York City and its ethnic neighborhoods, low-life character types, mundane scenes, alienation, and the rush of life. In March, 1931 MH wrote Harriet Monroe about the *Tompkins Square* poems, stating that they were "derived in essence from the attractive immigrant neighborhood I live in—handsome Poles and Lithuanians, Ukranians—& whatnot—with newspapers in all their languages" (letter to Harriet Monroe, University of Chicago, Special Collections). He was living at this time in Brooklyn, at the Pierrepont Hotel.

332

WINDOW WASHER—AVENUE C   First published in *Poetry*, 40 (April 1932), 23. Text source: *Tompkins Square Tabloids* typescript.

BULLDOG ON THE ROOF—AVENUE C   Unpublished. Text source: *Tompkins Square Tabloids* typescript.

KUZAN—FIRST AVENUE   Unpublished. Text source: *Tompkins Square Tabloids* typescript. Line 2, "myrrh" corrects MH's misspelling, "myhrr."

TWO WAYS OF LOVE   First published in SP, pp. 49–50. Text source: *Fifty-ninth Street Fables* typescript.

IN THOSE EXQUISITE AREAS   Unpublished. Text source: *Fifty-ninth Street Fables* typescript.

CITY VIGNETTES: MUSICOLOGIST—PREFERENCE, PROKO-FIEFF   Unpublished. Text source: *City Vignettes* typescript. See also the drawing of the same title (though mis-read as "Reference Prokofiev") in *Ninety-nine Drawings by Marsden Hartley* (Lewiston, Maine: Bates College Art Department, 1970), no. 15.

SHE SAUNTERED MOST ELEGANTLY DOWN   Unpublished. Text source: *City Vignettes* typescript.

DAILY LIBRARY VISITOR   First published in SP, p. 59; also published in *Marsden Hartley: Visionary of Maine* (Presque Isle, Maine: University of Maine, 1982, p. 3. Text source: *Gay World* typescript; second of three poems in a series with the same title.

WINDOW CLEANER TO NUDE MANIKIN   First published in SP, p. 93. Text source: *Gay World* typescript. Capitalization and question mark here have been added for clarity.

SWEET OLD MAN   Unpublished. Text source: *Gay World* typescript.

UN RECUERDO HERMANO—HART CRANE, R.I.P. (1932—33)

A footnote by MH at the end of the poem reads: "The bridge as symbol in repetition is used here because it was the end of Hart Crane's poetical effort, and he gave out more than once to us here in Mexico, the thought that he had nothing more to say."

MH and Crane had been friends for several years, having crossed paths in 1929 in Marseilles and seen each other frequently in Brooklyn in 1931. Crane's intensity and sociable camaraderie attracted the more shy and quiet MH. Thus Crane's suicide in April, 1932, deeply affected many people, including MH, who was among those who bade Crane farewell in Mexico City when he departed for New York.

Like others who were close to him during Crane's final days in Mexico—days that saw several suicide attempts and frenzied efforts to save the poet—part of MH's sense of loss stemmed from the feeling that it could have been prevented, that he and others might have been able to dissuade Crane from self-destruction if they had been with him on the voyage. MH wrote to a friend, just after hearing of the tragedy, that he could have saved Crane from "the final one . . . chiefly because I am steady & love the feeling of order in the mind. . . . I make a good shepherd you know and take care of my flock" (letter to Donald Greason, April 15, 1933 YCAL).

As with other sudden tragic losses in MH's life (the death in World War I of his friend Karl von Freyburg, the death of Alice Miriam, and the drowning of Alty and Donny Mason in Nova Scotia), Crane's death became, for MH, like the phoenix, generating new life in his creative work: specifically this poem, three essays (see "In Memoriam, Hart Crane" and two other unpublished essays, YCAL, and the painting *Eight Bells Folly*, 1933–34). A threnody, "Un Recuerdo Hermano—Hart Crane" (subtitled in one draft, "A Memory Brother or A Memory, Brother") was written while MH was still in Mexico—thus quite close to the event. The deep sense of pathos at the loss of both friend and poetic genius, the epigraphs from Jacopone da Todi and William Blake, and the emotional, personal intensity of the language of the poem, all suggest the shift that was taking place in MH's thought and poetic voice during that year in Mexico. The elegiac sweep of the lines stands in sharp contrast to the harsh, satiric tone of such earlier poems as the "Boston Portrait Projections" or the hard, taut lines of a poem like "The woman distorts, with hunger."

Unpublished. Text source: Hartley's typescript. A holograph draft version also exists, written in ink on pink and white paper. In the first epigraph "Jacopone" corrects MH's misspelling, "Jacoponi," and in the lines from Blake's poem, *The Book of Ahania*, punctuation and capitalization have been corrected to conform to the published version.

334

TANGENT DECISIONS (1935)

MH's typescript for this collection is inscribed "Completed in Bermuda 1935" where he had been to recuperate after a difficult winter in New York. The two epigraphs from Gérard de Nerval provide a key to the poems as well as to the whole thrust of MH's esthetic ideas at the time. The poems reveal his immersion in nature—"identifying" himself with "the infinite chain of created things." (See also his prose from the same period, particularly "Letter to Monsieur Dunoyer de Segonzac" in *Northern Lights Studies in Creativity*, University of Maine at Presque Isle, no. 1, 66–71, in which he refers to the same Nerval passage.) MH was discovering that the governing of dreams is achieved through a complete understanding of nature.

In "The Mystic Kneeling" the lines "Perfect stillness / Perfect fecundity" are an epigram by the thirteenth-century Flemish mystic Jan van Ruysbroeck, whom MH had been reading while in the Bavarian Alps in 1933–34. The "perfect stillness" needed for creativity is in contrast to the "battalions of words / too sumptuously spoken" at the end of "Stones to wind." See Gail Scott, "Marsden Hartley: Alspitz Mittenwald Road," *The Preston Morton Collection of American Art* (Santa Barbara Museum of Art, 1981), pp. 240–43.

Publication and text source: Those poems previously published are noted below. All texts are based on a forty-eight page typescript with corrections in Hartley's hand.

WEST CHEEK TO ROSE   First published in SP, p. 133. In the typescript version the word "mystica" in the final stanza is crossed out, and in MH's hand, it is written in *after* the word "rosa"—thus this change from the SP version.

HOLLANDER'S ANIMAL FAITH   First published in SP, pp. 41–43.

MIRACLE CARY AND HIS TWELVE LOAVES—TWELVE FISHES First published in SP, pp. 61–64.

SESTETS and SEA ENGRAVING—STYLE OF 1880   Variant typescripts of both these poems are found "Selected Poems from Unpublished MSS" (YCAL, Wells 7).

OCTOBER AFTERNOON (ca. 1937)

The title poem and several others in this undated collection (probably written sometime after 1937) concern a theme which dominates much of MH's late poetry: October (or sometimes September) as the month when summer finally fades and the seasons turn.

Publication and text source: Those poems previously published are noted below. All poems are based on the typescript MSS with corrections in MH's hand.

HOW LIKE THE SEA First published in SP, p. 97.

INVITATION First published in SP, pp. 87–88.

YESTERDAY, IN THE NIGHT First published in SP, pp. 110–11.

POT-LUCK AMONG THE CASUALS First published in SP, pp. 123–24.

LAUGHTER OF STEEL

MH worked on this MS on and off for a long time. He first mentions it in a letter to Stieglitz (YCAL, August 2, 1920) under the title "Laughter of Decision"—a two part autobiographical piece consisting of one part prose and one part poetry, "aimed at perfect satire" of the "vulgarity of American money aristocracy," and written with "metallic" violence of "words that pain." Later, in the 1930s he was still working on the MS recompiling it and including fifteen poems that are also in *Rites of Passage*.

Publication and text source: thirty-three page typescript; there is also a holograph version from a three ring notebook. Another twenty-two page typescript was typed by Norma Berger (YCAL, Wells 6a). Those poems previously published are noted below.

LAUGHTER OF STEEL Parts 1 and 2 first published in SP, pp. 67–68.

PISTOLS FOR PLEASURE—GUITARS FOR DEFENSE First published in SP, pp. 70–71.

A PRESENT TO THE SUN   First published in SP, p. 70.

SOLDIER ON HIS KNEES IN THE SNOW   First published in SP, pp. 68–69.

LIGHT-HEAVY AT PRAYER   Appears in two holograph versions—one in the *Laughter of Steel* notebook (which seems to be the second draft and is the text source used here), and the other among some miscellaneous holograph MSS (YCAL, Berger 35:2). In the latter the full title reads: "Light heavy—Acadian Yankee of Madawaska, Maine"; in the former, MH scratched out the second part of the title and inserted "at Prayer." In the winter of 1939, while living in Bangor, Maine, MH hired a young wrestler—an "Acadian Yankee" or American of French-Canadian heritage—from Madawaska, Maine, as a model. The next summer he painted a series of stunning portraits of male figures based on this model.

OBLIQUE FRONTIER

These poems were probably written and compiled in the late 1930s, but little else is known about the collection, except what can be inferred from its title (referring to the theme of death so pervasive in MH's late poetry) and other internal characteristics.

Publication and text source: Forty-one page typescript with corrections in MH's hand. Those poems previously published are noted below.

THIS LIVING IN SMALL PLACE   First published in *Androscoggin*, pp. 34–35.

WATCHING   First published in SP, p. 132.

OBLIQUE FRONTIER   First published in *Androscoggin*, p. 33; and SP, p. 5, under the title "Casual Frontier"; also published in *Marsden Hartley: Visionary of Maine*, p. 3. In the typescript, the word "Casual" is crossed out and "Oblique" inserted in MH's hand; thus the present text conforms to the original typescript.

PERHAPS MACABRE   First published in SP, pp. 94–95, where the subtitle "(to Georgia O'Keeffe)" was added; since it does not appear in the original MS, it has been omitted here. The reference to

Georgia O'Keeffe is, however, unmistakable, the "she" of the poem no doubt being the wife of Stieglitz and friend and colleague of MH. (See his essay, "Georgia O'Keeffe — A Second Outline in Portraiture," in *On Art*, pp. 102–08.) Mention of animal skeletons and roses seen against the sky evokes images of O'Keeffe's numerous paintings of cow or ram skulls, with a flower, on a field of blue sky.

TRAPEZIST'S DESPAIR   Concerns the circus performer Alfredo Codona who in 1937 shot his wife, Vera Bruce, and then killed himself. He had earlier been married to the trapezist, Lillian Leitzel who was killed in a fall in 1931. MH, who was a lifelong circus-goer, followed the careers of Codona and Leitzel and, after meeting them in New York (probably in 1928 shortly before they were married), wrote about them on several occasions. (See the unpublished essay: "Two Great Circus Artists — Lillian Leitzel and Alfredo Codona" YCAL.)

HE TOO WORE A BUTTERFLY   First published in SP, pp. 95–96.

FOR GASTON LACHAISE — A SORT OF WRITTEN FRIEZE Concerns MH's friend, the sculptor, Gaston Lachaise to whom he had also written a tribute in the essay "Thinking of Gaston Lachaise," (*On Art*, pp. 282–86). Line 16, "rosace" is the French word for a stained glass rose window.

NEW RAINS WASH DOWN

Although this collection was probably compiled in the late 1930s, several poems were written as early as 1931.

Publication and text source: Thirty-one page typescript with corrections in MH's hand. Poems previously published are noted below.

SOLILOQUY IN DOGTOWN — CAPE ANN   Written probably during or sometime shortly after MH's visit to Dogtown Common, near Gloucester, Massachusetts, in 1931. The poem relates to the series of paintings he executed there, specifically *Flaming Pool*, on the reverse of which is inscribed what may be a preliminary version of this poem, titled "Beethoven (in Dogtown)":

> Deep chested trills arise —
> from organ pipes of juniper
> Oboe's throat expands — mezzo cries

338

of blueberry and sage and ferns prefer
to die among the rocks, nobly perish
mire of torid green-
Summer's strident blades of damascene
hot tone or here is garish
the vox humana swells and dwells
Persistently mid nuances of lapis grey
So much more wonderful this way
than summer in a trance
of chlorophyll or other circumstances

See Gail R. Scott, "Marsden Hartley at Dogtown Common," *Arts
Magazine* 54 (October 1979), 159–65; and *Marsden Hartley: Solilo-
quy in Dogtown* exhibition catalogue (Cape Ann, Massachusetts:
Cape Ann Historical Association, 1985), p. 23.

ALICE MIRIAM   Unpublished. Refers to an aspiring young opera
singer who was a close friend of MH from 1912 until her death
in 1922. She was engaged to the German sculptor, Arnold
Rönnebeck with whom MH stayed on various trips to Europe. She
died suddenly of appendicitis in 1922, and shortly thereafter MH
wrote a poem, now lost, entitled "Alias Tommy" (his pet name for
her). See also the unpublished essay, "Letter to Alice Miriam,"
YCAL.

GEOMETRIC DEATH   First published in SP, pp. 112–13, where
Wells added the subtitle "Still Life."

KING AMENEMHAT III, QUEEN NEFERTITI—SMALL FRAG-
MENT OF NOSE AND MOUTH ONLY, and SAME FRAGMENT
—SECOND LOOK   When he was in New York, MH used to spend
many hours in the Metropolitan Museum of Art where he especially enjoyed the Egyptian rooms, and in 1931 he must have purchased
photographs of these fragments of Egyptian sculpture which inspired the poems (see illustrations, following p. 160). In August,
1931 he wrote to a friend that he had nothing in his room to look
at except these three photographs. The Queen Nefertiti piece, he
commented, was "such a fine piece of sensuality" while the King
Amenemhat had ". . . a magnificent axe-grinding nose" and all were
"the most superb things I've encountered lately. . . . I love the Egyptian stuff at the Met [for] their coolness, their superb contempt
for personality and all the riff-raff of egotism that gets called art
these days" (letter to Rebecca Strand, August 3, 1931, from
Gloucester, Mass., YCAL). MH's copies of these photographs

are among his memorabilia at the Treat Gallery, Bates College. According to the most recent research at the Metropolitan Museum, the Nefertiti piece is now considered to be actually King Akhenaton, husband of Nefertiti—an interesting note in view of MH's references to the sexuality in the fragments, and his admiration for androgynous sensuality. MH's spelling of Amenemhat has been corrected. "Queen Nefertiti—Small Fragment of Nose and Mouth Only" was first published in SP, pp. 114–15.

M.T.—A RELATIVE IN CERTAIN ASPECTS OF METAPHYS-ICAL DIVINATION   Refers to Mark Tobey, fellow painter and friend, in whom MH found a sympathetic soul in matters relating to mysticism and the occult. See "Mark Tobey," in *On Art*, pp. 182–85; 297–98.

WINGAERSHEEK BEACH   First published in SP, p. 131. Wingaer-sheek Beach is near Gloucester, Massachusetts.

NEW RAINS WASH DOWN   Refers to the many four- and five-masted ships lying unused in such New England ports as Wisscaset and Gloucester.

RITES OF PASSAGE

Publication and text source: Holograph originals in black leather three ring binder. These poems were later typed by Norma Berger; MH appears to have selected a few of these poems and typed them himself, perhaps to submit them for publication consideration. Poems previously published are noted below.

SURPRISE PACKAGE   First published in SP, p. 137.

YIELDING THE INITIATIVE   A different poem by the same title appears in the MS of *Oblique Frontier* (YCAL, Wells 10, 36).

JOHN DONNE IN HIS SHROUD   First published in SP, pp. 104–05. There is also a painting, executed in 1940, *The Last Look of John Donne*. Donne was one of MH's favorite poets; his library (part of the Memorial Collection at Bates College) contains a number of books of Donne's poetry.

AMERICAN IKON—LINCOLN   First published in SP, p. 48; another typescript is found in *Laughter of Steel* (YCAL, Wells 6,

26). (See Gail R. Scott, " 'The Surface of his Dignities,' " *The Christian Science Monitor*, February 10, 1977, p. 28; and Hartley's portraits of Abraham Lincoln, *Young Worshipper of the Truth, The Great Good Man*, and *Weary of the Truth* from the late '30s.

V—IS FOR VICTORY AS YOU CAN PLAINLY SEE   First published in SP, p. 74.

8 WORDS   First published in SP, p. 87; a different typescript also found in the *Laughter of Steel* MS (YCAL, Wells 6, 30).

IF IT WERE THE EYE   First published in *Laughter of Steel* MS (YCAL, Wells 6, 21), but without a title.

A WORD AND ITS MEANING   First published in SP, pp. 108–09. This poem, like "Yielding the Initiative" and several others, concerns MH's poetics—that is, his desire to follow Yeats' admonition to "yield the initiative to the word." (See the unpublished essay, "A Pope and a Poet," written in 1939 upon the death of William Butler Yeats, YCAL.)

DUSTY COUSIN

The epigraph to the collection as well as to the first poem, "There are no names" is from Paul Valéry, and dates this collection, for it was in 1939 that Hartley was reading the French author and quoting him often in his essays. (See "The Element of Absolutism in Leonardo's Drawings" in *On Art*, pp. 286–92, 303.

Publication and text source: Holograph originals in a spiral notebook. These poems were later typed by Norma Berger. Poems previously published are noted below.

VAST ROSE OF JULY   First published in SP, pp. 137–38. Line 7, the word "orients" corrects "variety"; the poem is untitlted in the holograph original.

LOGIC   First published in SP, p. 108.

PLOVER   First published in SP, p. 35. There are a number of paintings depicting dead sea birds—plovers, gulls and ducks; Hartley would beachcomb in Maine and Nova Scotia, bringing home shells, rope fragments and other seawashed remnants which would become subjects for both poems and paintings.

THIS MILLIMETER   First published in SP, p. 134.

WHOEVER DIES—DIES FOR THE LOVE   First published in SP, p. 117.

LITTLE GREEN SNAKE   First published in SP, pp. 109–10.

COURAGE FOR LOST POEMS   First published in SP, pp. 124–25.

MISCELLANEOUS LATE POEMS

The last six or seven years of MH's life were richly productive ones in both writing and painting. Besides the two books of poetry published by Leon Tebbetts in 1940 and 1941, and several collections of unpublished verse, there were numerous miscellaneous, uncollected poems—some handwritten, some written in notebooks and on loose leaves. The poems in this section are drawn from the following disparate MS sources: "New Poems" (YCAL, Wells 16), autostat originals in a blue Security writing tablet; "New Poems" (YCAL, Wells 17), autostat originals in a brown Gyral notebook; "Poems" (YCAL, Wells 20), autostat originals in a 8½" x 11" three-ring black leather notebook; "Poems (1938)" (YCAL, Wells 21), autostat originals in a small spiral notebook; "New Poems" (YCAL, Wells 23), autostat originals in a Security writing tablet; "Contrapuntal, a New Book of Poems" (1942) (YCAL, Wells 11), typescript originals; "Cleophas and His Own" (YCAL, Berger 31); a folder of loose autostat originals (YCAL, Berger 35:1); and a folder of miscellaneous notes, poems and fragments (YCAL, Berger 15). Many of these holograph collections were typed by Norma Berger (after MH's death), but the text sources for all poems are MH's handwritten or typed originals.

YES, I KNOW—YES   (Wells 16). Unpublished.

AT HALF PAST ANYTHING   (Wells 16). First published in SP, p. 20.

CICADA   (Wells 16). Unpublished.

REFLEX   (Wells 16). First published in SP, p. 19; also published in *Marsden Hartley: Visionary of Maine*, p. 2.

AND NOW—SEPTEMBER   (Wells 16). First published in SP, pp. 37–38.

THE FLIGHT   (Wells 16). First published in SP, p. 123.

WORD ARRANGEMENTS FOR PICTURES BY MORRIS GRAVES (Wells 16); the original MS includes seven poems under the title "Seven Word Arrangements for Pictures by Morris Graves"; three are included in the present edition. The poems were undoubtedly inspired by a group exhibition *Americans 1942* at the Museum of Modern Art in New York, 1942—the catalogue of which is among the books in MH's library at Bates College. Among the Graves paintings in the exhibition are all those on which MH based his "Word Arrangements."

LITTLE BIRD ALONE   Unpublished.

EAGLE OF THE INNER EYE   First published in SP, p. 112.

LITTLE KNOWN BIRD OF THE INNER EYE   Unpublished.

BUTTONS FOR SWALLOWS   (Wells 16). First published in SP, p. 96. As if to attempt to replicate the family button bag referred to in this poem, MH kept a collection of buttons, now found in MHMC.

ICHNEUMON   (Wells 16). First published in SP, pp. 135–36.

THIS PIECE OF EUCHARIST   (Wells 16). First published in SP, pp. 132–33. Line 8, by "anlage" (German: arrangement, layout) MH means, the low rise of land.

IMMORTAL FACE   (Wells 16). First published in SP, pp. 116–17.

K. VON F.—1914—ARRAS-BOUQUOI   (Wells 7). Unpublished. Concerns the death in one of the early battles of World War I, of Karl von Freyberg, who was Arnold Rönnebeck's cousin and close friend and lover of MH. (See the series of paintings on the theme of the "Portrait of a German Officer" 1914–15, in *Marsden Hartley* by Barbara Haskell, New York: Whitney Museum of American Art, 1981.)

FIND THE FACE   (Wells 16). First published in SP, pp. 74–75.

IT WAS TO LEARN   (Wells 17). Unpublished.

BLESSED EVENT   (Wells 20). Unpublished.

SEVERAL PIECES FOR JOSE GARCIA VILLA   (Wells 16). The original MS is divided into five short poems. Parts 1 and 5 were first published in SP, pp. 106–07 (numbered 1 and 2). The present

343

text selects the same two poems. MH read Villa's first book, *Have Come, Am Here* (New York: Viking Press, 1942) when it came out and met Villa in the winter of 1942–43. Villa apparently read some of MH's poetry, and, according to MH, liked it very much (letter to Adelaide Kuntz, n.d., Archives of American Art).

ALBERT RYDER – MOONLIGHTIST (Wells 16). First published in SP, p. 111. Ryder is another figure about whom MH wrote and painted a great deal. See his essays, "Ryder," in AIA, pp. 37–41; "Eakins, Homer, Ryder" and "Albert Pinkham Ryder" in *On Art*, pp. 168–72, 297; 256–68, 301; as well as several other unpublished essays and fragments in the YCAL; and his *Portrait of Albert Pinkham Ryder* (1938–39).

EILSHEMIUS (Wells 16). Unpublished. Refers to the eccentric and visionary American artist, Louis Eilshemius (1864–1941), whose work was championed and exhibited by the Société Anonyme in 1920 (the same year that MH was involved with the dadaist group; see also the unpublished essay by MH, "Louis Eilshemius" (YCAL).

MARIANNE MOORE (Wells 16). First published in SP, p. 111. In 1937 Marianne Moore read two poetry MSS of MH's: *Pressing Foot* (no longer extant as a collection) and *Tangent Decisions*. After giving him a brief critique and some encouragement, she sent them with her recommendation first to the *Atlantic Monthly* and then to *The Nation*, but without result. The MSS then went to *Poetry* where three poems were accepted, only to be later rejected after a change in editorship. MH was nevertheless honored and gratified by Moore's interest in his work. Moore later corresponded with Henry Wells regarding MH's poetry and encouraging its publication.

CONCERT (Berger 35:2). Unpublished.

HEIFETZ – ON THE AIR (Wells 16). Unpublished.

LISTENING TO THE MUSIC (Wells 17). First published in SP, p. 138.

WE HAVE BROKEN BREAD (Wells 17). Unpublished.

MOLE (Wells 17). First published in SP, p. 125.

TO PARTRIDGE MERRITHEW (Wells 17). Unpublished.

THE VERY LANGUOR (Wells 22). Unpublished.

344

SERVING THE CURVE   (Wells 23). Unpublished.

INNER DISTANCE   (Wells 20). Unpublished.

ENCOMPASSED   (Wells 20). Unpublished.

THREE LOVING MEN   (Wells 20). Unpublished. This poem, "Two Drowned at the Gateway," p. 263, "Two Lovely Ones," p. 266, and "Fishermen's Last Supper," p. 271, refer to the drowning in Nova Scotia of Alty and Donny Mason, with their cousin, in 1936 while MH was staying with the family. The gateway is a stretch of dangerous, rock-strewn water between Blue Rocks—the nearest town—and Eastern Point Island where the Masons lived. The bodies of the boys were found here after a severe hurricane struck the area. See also *Cleophas and His Own: A North Atlantic Tragedy* (Halifax, Nova Scotia: Nova Scotia College of Art and Design, 1982) which is a prose poem MH wrote in 1936 after the accident occurred, recounting his life with the Masons and the events of the drowning. Adelard and Etienne are MH's fictitious names for the boys.

O BITTER MADRIGAL   (Wells 20). First published in SP, pp. 75–76. Also the title of a drawing and painting (1942) MH made depicting a pietà subject with a woman holding the body of a youth; on her shoulder is a bird—whispering the madrigal.

FANTASY AND PHANTOM   (Berger 35:2). Unpublished.

THERE ARE NO ROCKS AND TREES   (Contrapuntal, Berger 3). Unpublished.

PERUSING MALLARMÉ IN MAINE   (Berger 15). First published in SP, p. 103. MH mentions in several letters from Georgetown, Maine in 1937 that he was reading Mallarmé; the poem again quotes the line "yielding the initiative."

RECOGNITION OF REGION   (Berger 15). Unpublished.

BACK ROAD COUNTRY   (Berger 35:1). Unpublished.

BEYOND THE BROKEN HOUSE   (Berger 35:1). Unpublished.

THE PILGRIMAGE, AND THE GAME WARDEN   (Berger 35:1). Unpublished. Concerns MH's trip to Katahdin Lake in Maine in October 1939 to paint Mt. Katahdin. He was taken by Maine State

Game Warden, Caleb Warren Scribner. See also the unpublished essay in "Be that as It May," (YCAL) and the many paintings of the mountain that he did in subsequent years. MH here employs the Indian spelling of Mt. Katahdin (used also by Henry David Thoreau).

"WHAT HAVE WE ALL—" (Berger 35:1). Unpublished.

VESPER HYMN FOR TUESDAY AND JUNE (Berger 35:1 holograph original). Unpublished. MH's close friend, Adelaide Kuntz, introduced him to Henry Wells who taught poetry at Columbia University—hoping that Wells might help in the effort to publish MH's poetry. Katharine Wells recalls a visit by MH in late May or June, 1943, to their home in Riverdale to discuss his poetry. She says, "We walked together downhill to the local railroad station at Spuyten Duyvil where I realized that I had misread the timetable and we had a half hour to wait—which we did, sitting on a bench by full moonlight watching the currents from the Hudson River seep along the Ship Canal Inlet" (letter to the editor, July 24, 1982). This could well have been the visit that inspired the poem. MH was very encouraged by Wells' interest in his poetry. Two drafts of an article by Wells on the poetry are in the Bates College Special Collections, and MH's letters to Wells express appreciation for the professor's flattering remarks in the article. (See Wells' article, "The Poetry of Marsden Hartley," *Quarterly Review of Literature*, 2:1 [Winter 1944], 100–107.) Stanza 3, line 7, "breeze" is my reading of a difficult-to-decipher word.

TO THE NAMELESS ONE (Berger 35:1). Unpublished.

REMBRANDT—ROUAULT—PIERO (Wells 31). Unpublished. These are three of MH's favorite painters about whom he has written individual essays; see *On Art*, pp. 122–25; 213–17; 116–17; 223; 263.

ANDROSCOGGIN (1940)

MH's first book of poems in 17 years, *Androscoggin* was published by Falmouth Publishing House, Portland, Maine, a small press owned by Leon Tebbetts and devoted primarily to Maine authors. Two of MH's poems had appeared in another Falmouth book, *The Triad Anthology of New England Verse* (ed. Louise Hall Littlefield, 1938), so Tebbetts was already familiar with his work, when they met through the poet Harold Vinal, whose work

346

Tebbetts also published. *Androscoggin* came about partially as a result of MH's determination at this particular juncture to become fully identified with his native state and become its poet laureate. He actively sought publication exposure in Maine.

The original MS for *Androscoggin* has not survived intact, and it is not known how MH compiled the poems for this book. Many of them exist only in the published form. A few original typescripts have survived, scattered among the YCAL MSS. Where a typescript or autostat original exists, it will be noted below; otherwise the text follows the 1940 published version, except for punctuation, capitalization and italics as discussed in the Preface.

Publication: Only those poems published elsewhere besides *Androscoggin* are noted below.

RETURN OF THE NATIVE   First published in *Contact*, n.s. 2 (May 1932), 28; and subsequently in *Pictures of New England by a New Englander* (exhibition catalogue, New York: The Downtown Gallery, 1932), p. 2; SP, p. 3; *Marsden Hartley: Visionary of Maine*; *Marsden Hartley: Soliloquy in Dogtown*, p. 1; and in numerous other publications. The poem, written just after MH's return from nearly a decade in Europe, is a poetic evocation of his intention to come home to his native New England.

ANDROSCOGGIN   Also published in SP, pp. 9–10.

LEWISTON IS A PLEASANT PLACE   Also published in SP, pp. 10–13. A typescript version exists among the papers of Arthur Plummer, a friend of MH from Lewiston (Kent State University Library, Special Collections). The typescript version has been followed, omitting the italics of "The Children of the Sun," stanza 9, line 9, which appear in the *Androscoggin* version.

FAMILY ALBUM IN RED PLUSH   Also published in SP, pp. 13–15. As with the above poem, there is a typescript copy of "Family Album" among the Arthur Plummer papers (Kent State University Library) which is used for the present text. Stanza 1, line 9, corrects the misspelling of "Staylybridge" in the *Androscoggin* version. Stanza 2, lines 14 and 16, the italics have been omitted from the titles "The Rivals," "Rip Van Winkle," "Nick of the Woods," and "Fanchon the Cricket." Stanza 5, line 1, upper case on Republican.

THE BEND OF THE ANDROSCOGGIN   Also published in SP, p. 8.

ELIAS GOVE – OR, THE SECOND COMING   Also published in SP, pp. 50–51.

TWO DROWNED AT THE GATEWAY   Also published in SP, pp. 32–33. Original typescript (YCAL, Berger 35:2).

THE OUTCAST CITY ON THE KENNEBEC   Also published in SP, pp. 15–17. Original typescript (YCAL, Berger 35:2).

TWO LOVELY ONES   Also published in SP, pp. 31–32.

ISLANDS IN PENOBSCOT BAY   Also published in SP, pp. 5–7. See also the series of paintings of the same title.

FISHERMAN'S LAST SUPPER   Also published in SP, p. 30. A slightly longer version of the same poem is in *Cleophas and His Own*. See also the painting of the same title.

THESE SIX OR SEVERAL HOUSES   Also published in SP, pp. 17–18.

THERE IS AN ISLAND   Also published in SP, p. 18.

ROBIN HOOD COVE – GEORGETOWN, MAINE   Also published in SP, pp. 19–20. See also the painting of the same title.

A. LINCOLN – ODD, OR EVEN   Also published in SP, pp. 46–47.

THIS PORTRAIT OF A SEADOVE, DEAD   First published in *Marsden Hartley: First Exhibition in Four Years* (New York: An American Place, 1936) exhibition catalogue; and also in SP, pp. 34–35. Variant original versions also collected by Hartley in *Fifty-ninth Street Fables* and "Selected Poems from Unpublished MSS." The American Place catalogue version is used here; it has no stanza break or quotation marks, and "seadove" is one word. The *Androscoggin* version misprinted "grave" for "brave," line 14.

THIS CRUSTY FRAGMENT   Also published in SP, pp. 113–14 where the subtitle "Still Life" was added. A typescript original with the title "As it says in the papers" is found in YCAL, Berger 35:2.

THE BERRY HOUSE   First published in *The Triad Anthology of New England Verse*, pp. 32–33; and also in SP, pp. 88–89. Original typescript in YCAL, Berger 35:2. "Newman" (line 4) was Roy Newman, MH's friend. From a letter to Newman (January 17, 1941, YCAL), it is apparent that the idea for the poem arose after a walk they took together in Georgetown, Maine in the summer of 1937.

SEA BURIAL (1941)

Androscoggin sold out its 300 copies almost immediately, and in 1941 Tebbetts agreed to publish another volume of MH's poetry, SB. Whereas *Androscoggin* was a cohesive group of poems encompassing the Maine of Hartley's origin and of his return, SB is broad in its scope. It attempts to bring together the opposite halves of MH's experience—his cosmopolitan need of the city, of music, literature and things intellectual, with the simplicity of plain people and isolated nature. As a book SB lacked the firm, lean thrust of the earlier volume, though there are many fine poems in the collection. This selection from the book culls out the most successful of the poems.

Unlike *Androscoggin*, a typescript (complete except for one poem) does exist for SB, though there are discrepancies. The title page is signed in MH's hand, "Completed Feb. 6, 1941 Bangor, Maine Marsden Hartley." None of the poems in SB exist in other collections or other typescript versions, and none was previously published, although those published in SP are noted below. The text source for all but one poem is MH's typescript, and all words printed in italics in both the SB and SP versions have been restored to all upper case letters as the poet typed them. Poems published elsewhere are noted below.

CONFIDENCE   Also published in SP, p. 121.

IN ROBIN HOOD COVE   Also published in SP, p. 3.

THE LONELY RETURN TO THE LONELY   Also published in SP, p. 129, where the subtitle "The divine to the Divine—Proclus" was omitted.

INDIAN POINT   Also published in SP, p. 4. Line 1 in both the SB and SP versions has "licks" where MH's typescript has "licking."

CYRIAQUE D'ETREMONT   Also published in SP, pp. 46–47, where the subtitle "Bluenose Portrait Effect #1" was omitted. The term "bluenose" as used by Mainers, is a nickname for Nova Scotians, supposedly reflecting the rigors of their climate, though, according to philologists, it actually refers to the type of bluish potatoes peculiar to the province. It also has a slightly deprecating connotation when applied by Maine fishermen to their northern competitors—a meaning probably not intended by MH, who admired the hardy fishermen of both Maine and Nova Scotia. He undoubtedly wished to stress the more general meaning of standing vigorously for a certain moral code.

BLAIR PURVES   Also published in SP, pp. 43–45 where again, the subtitle was omitted, and the order of the two "portraits" was reversed. "Massaquodaboit" is MH's spelling for Musquodoboit, Nova Scotia. The inspiration for these two portraits may well have come from people he met during his two summers in Nova Scotia, 1935 and 1936.

IF WE COULD   Also published in SP, p. 130 where stanza 2, line 1 misprints "I" for "we."

ANY PAGE OF THOMAS MANN'S   Also published in SP, p. 104, where line 8 dropped "like."

WHAT IS SACRAMENT   Also published in SP, p. 83. Both the SP and SB versions inserted a question mark on the title, which does not appear in the typescript.

AS THE BUCK LAY DEAD   Also published in SP, p. 36.

RICHARD ROLLE   Also published in SP, pp. 134–35.

HOROWITZ   Also published in SP, pp. 115–16.

GIANT AND SON   MH's typescript for this poem is missing; thus the published version stands.

BE THAT AS IT MAY (1941)

The MS of this collection consists of autostat originals of both prose and poetry in a black leather notebook, the title page of which is inscribed by MH "Fort Tryon Park Easter 1941." As in many of his late collections, the subjects of these pieces shift back and forth between city scenes and Maine themes, reflecting his habit in the later years of spending most winters in New York and the summers in Maine. Poems published elsewhere are noted below.

OLD LADY IN THE PARK   First published in SP, pp. 58–59.

THE LADIES AND THE PIGEONS   First published in SP, pp. 58–59.

FURNISHED ROOMS   A different poem with the same title was published in SB, pp. 41–42.

A GOING MAN   First published in SP, p. 49. In the autostat MS the subtitle "Stieglitz" has been crossed out—probably by MH, although the poem was most likely occasioned by Stieglitz's illnesses in the late 1930s and early '40s. A different, but related poem, "A Man—Going to Pieces" was published in *Androscoggin*, pp. 28–29.

THREE FRIENDS   Also published in SP, pp. 98–99. See also the drawing and painting of the same title.

PATTERNS FOR PRAYERS

Not much is known about this short collection of poems, except that the autostat MS appears to have been written sometime after 1940. None of the poems was published, nor was the MS ever typed by MH or Norma Berger; it was not submitted to Henry Wells as part of the collected poetry to be considered for inclusion in SP.

Text source: Twenty-one page holograph MS, transcribed by the editor.

On the Business of Poetry

First published in *Poetry* (vol. 15, no. 111, Dec. 1919, pp. 152–158). The years 1918–1919 mark Hartley's debut as a published poet, twice in *Poetry*, in *The Little Review*, in several issues of Alfred Kreymborg's *Others for 1919: An Anthology of the New Verse*, and in two issues of *Playboy: Magazine of Art and Satire*. And in 1919 Harriet Monroe published "The Business of Poetry," Hartley's only statement of poetics. Though he had been writing poetry and essays on poetry for many years and associating with numerous poets and literary circles both in America and in Europe, it was only in this post-war period that he actively sought and first achieved publication.

He wrote the essay late in 1919 while, as he says, "riding through Arizona on the Pullman" on his return to New York after a year and a half in New Mexico and California. He must have given the essay to Monroe when he stopped over in Chicago on this return train ride.

In Los Angeles earlier that year, he had attended several poetry gatherings where he had given his first reading of his own work. Present at one of these occasions was Robert McAlmon, a flamboyant young poet-aviator whose first poems, "Aero-Laughter," "Aero-Metre," and others had struck Hartley when they appeared in *Poetry* in the March 1919 issue. The intensity of the poems revealed McAlmon's eager grasp of the emerging new technical era, in the spirit (wholly American) of the current Futurist movement. The two struck up a friendship, and Hartley promised to introduce McAlmon to his New York poet friends when the latter came East. This he did, with the resulting collaboration between William Carlos Williams, McAlmon and Hartley on the first issue of *Contact*, in which these same ideas of a poetics of immediate experience came to a focus. But in the meantime, this initial meeting stimulated Hartley's thought about the purpose of poetry, generating this essay. "The Business of Poetry" captures the dynamics and energy of McAlmon's poetry and also uses images from aviation and the mechanical world to describe the future of poetry. It can be compared to Hartley's essay "Dissertation on Modern Painting" (*On Art*, pp. 68–70), written two years later, which discusses the need in both the poetry and art of modern America to "be drawn out of life itself" and to be "a matter of direct contact" with the "mechanistic brilliance and precision of this era."

Index of Titles and First Lines

Printed November 1986 in Santa Barbara &
Ann Arbor for the Black Sparrow Press by
Graham Mackintosh & Edwards Brothers Inc.
Design by Barbara Martin. This edition
is published in paper wrappers; there are
300 hardcover trade copies; 150 hardcover
copies have been numbered & signed by the
editor; & 26 copies handbound in boards by
Earle Gray have been lettered & signed by
the editor.

GAIL SCOTT (b. 1943) received her Master's Degree in art history from the University of California, Berkeley in 1967. From 1967 to 1972 she was Assistant Curator of Modern Art at the Los Angeles County Museum of Art. In 1977 she was awarded a three year Research Grant from the National Endowment for the Humanities to edit the poetry and prose of Marsden Hartley. After moving to northern Maine in 1981, she organized an exhibition of Hartley's painting and poetry of Maine shown at the University of Maine at Presque Isle and other locations in the state. She is a free lance writer, teaches occasional art history courses, and is currently at work on a monograph on Hartley's painting.

MARSDEN HARTLEY was born in 1877 in Lewiston, Maine. At the age of 14 he left school and went to work in a shoe factory. The next year he joined his family which had moved to Cleveland, Ohio. There he studied art with several different teachers, and in 1898 he received a five year stipend to continue his art training in New York City, first at the William Merritt Chase School, and then at the National Academy of Design. During these years he spent his summers in Maine, painting its landscape and writing poetry. In 1908 Alfred Stieglitz gave him his first one-man exhibition and took him into his stable of artists at the famed 291 Gallery. Between 1912 and 1916, and again from 1922 to 1929, Hartley lived primarily in Europe where he travelled, painted and wrote.

In 1918 Hartley began to publish—both poetry and essays— in many of the leading periodicals of his day, including *The Dial, Poetry, The Little Review, Contact, American Caravan* and *Others.* His first book—essays on art, literature and vaudeville— *Adventures in the Arts* appeared in 1921. Three volumes of his verse were published during his lifetime: *Twenty-five Poems* (1925); *Androscoggin* (1940); and *Sea Burial* (1941).

Hartley continued to exhibit his paintings at Alfred Stieglitz's An American Place and Intimate Galleries, and later with other New York dealers. In 1930 he received a Guggenheim Fellowship for which he travelled in Mexico (1932–33), followed by four months in Germany. Returning to America in 1934, he devoted himself with renewed energy in poetry and painting to the place of his origin, New England, and especially his native Maine. He died in Corea, Maine in 1943.

He has had several retrospective painting exhibitions—at the Museum of Modern Art in 1944, the Stedelijk Museum, Amsterdam in 1961, and, most recently, the Whitney Museum of American Art in 1980; his paintings are in the collections of major museums all over the world. In 1945 Henry Wells edited a collection of his poetry, *Selected Poems;* and in 1982 Gail Scott published an edition of his essays, *On Art.*